Making Evaluation Research Useful to Congress

Leonard Saxe, Daniel Koretz, *Editors*

NEW DIRECTIONS FOR PROGRAM EVALUATION
A Publication of the Evaluation Research Society
SCARVIA B. ANDERSON, *Editor-in-Chief*

Number 14, June,1982

Paperback sourcebooks in
The Jossey-Bass Higher Education and
Social and Behavioral Sciences Series

62985

Jossey-Bass Inc., Publishers
San Francisco • Washington • London

Making Evaluation Research Useful to Congress
Number 14, June 1982
    Leonard Saxe, Daniel Koretz, *Editors*

New Directions for Program Evaluation Series
A Publication of the Evaluation Research Society
Scarvia B. Anderson, *Editor-in-Chief*

New Directions for Program Evaluation (publication number
USPS 449-050) is published quarterly by Jossey-Bass Inc.,
Publishers, and is sponsored by the Evaluation Research Society.
Second-class postage rates paid at San Francisco, California,
and at additional mailing offices.

Correspondence:
Subscriptions, single-issue orders, change of address notices,
undelivered copies, and other correspondence should be sent to
New Directions Subscriptions, Jossey-Bass Inc., Publishers,
433 California Street, San Francisco, California 94104.

Editorial correspondence should be sent to the Editor-in-Chief,
Scarvia B. Anderson, Educational Testing Service, 250 Piedmont
Avenue, Suite 2020, Atlanta, Georgia 30308.

Library of Congress Catalogue Card Number LC 81-48578
International Standard Serial Number ISSN 0164-7989
International Standard Book Number ISBN 87589-916-1

Cover art by Willi Baum
Manufactured in the United States of America

Ordering Information

The paperback sourcebooks listed below are published quarterly and can be ordered either by subscription or as single copies.

Subscriptions cost $35.00 per year for institutions, agencies, and libraries. Individuals can subscribe at the special rate of $21.00 per year *if payment is by personal check.* (Note that the full rate of $35.00 applies if payment is by institutional check, even if the subscription is designated for an individual.) Standing orders are accepted.

Single copies are available at $7.95 when payment accompanies order, and *all single-copy orders under $25.00 must include payment.* (California, Washington, D.C., New Jersey, and New York residents please include appropriate sales tax.) For billed orders, cost per copy is $7.95 plus postage and handling. (Prices subject to change without notice.)

To ensure correct and prompt delivery, all orders must give either the *name of an individual* or an *official purchase order number.* Please submit your order as follows:

Subscriptions: specify series and subscription year.
Single Copies: specify sourcebook code and issue number (such as, PE8).

Mail orders for United States and Possessions, Latin America, Canada, Japan, Australia, and New Zealand to:
Jossey-Bass Inc., Publishers
433 California Street
San Francisco, California 94104

Mail orders for all other parts of the world to:
Jossey-Bass Limited
28 Banner Street
London EC1Y 8QE

New Directions for Program Evaluation Series
Scarvia B. Anderson, *Editor-in-Chief*

Contents

Editors' Notes

To the extent that the ultimate goal of evaluation research is to contribute to the formation of policy, the U.S. Congress is potentially one of its most crucial audiences. To date, however, the contributions of evaluation research to congressional deliberations have been modest at best. Cultivating the Congress as an audience for evaluation and making evaluation research more useful to the Congress are critical tasks if evaluation research is to manifest its potential for informing policy.

The goal of the chapters in this volume is to clarify some issues concerning congressional use of evaluation. Each chapter describes how evaluation research was used in congressional deliberations on a particular set of issues. As a group, the chapters provide a perspective —and some concrete suggestions—that should be helpful to researchers who would like to increase the usefulness of their work in the policy-making process.

The authors of the chapters have an informed perspective on the workings of the Congress. All are social scientists and evaluators who worked on Capitol Hill as Congressional Science Fellows some time during the period 1978–1980, under the sponsorship of either a congressional agency or a professional society. All were participants in the Congressional Science Fellowship program of the American Association for the Advancement of Science (AAAS). Their experiences in the Congress differed, however, not only because of their varied responsibilities as congressional staff but also because of their varied disciplinary backgrounds. Although the chapters discuss the Congress in general, each is based on and clearly colored by the author's specific experiences.

The Congressional Context in 1978–1980

To put the chapters into perspective, some general comments on the nature of the Congress are needed. The U.S. Congress has become organizationally more complex and has grown rapidly in recent years. By 1978, the institution of Congress included not only the 535 elected members but also staff and support agency personnel totaling about 40,000 people. The existence of large congressional staff and support agencies has had a dramatic impact on the operations of Congress (Fox and Hammond, 1977). For evaluation research, this growth in staff has meant that Congress has additional means of

1

using the information generated by research in legislative deliberations.

Recent years have also seen a shift in emphasis in congressional activities. In many committees, the design and establishment of new programs have become somewhat less central; in their place has come a growing concern with oversight and with the refinement and modification of existing programs. (For a discussion of changes in congressional oversight, see Aherback, 1979.) For example, many of the major social programs, such as Medicare, Medicaid, and Title I compensatory education, have been in existence for a decade and a half. Since their establishment, the relevant committees of the Congress have spent a great deal of time and effort assessing these programs and deciding whether and how to modify them. Although the Congress's methods of assessing these programs are often very different from those that an evaluator might envision, as the chapters in this issue attest, this change in emphasis greatly increases the potential role of evaluation research in the legislative process.

In order to understand the functioning of this now very large organization, it is helpful to conceptualize the Congress as a series of concentric circles. The inner circle is the members of both Houses, organized into a complex array of overlapping committees and subcommittees. Most of the Congress's work is done in the committees and subcommittees, and even when the House or Senate is working as a unitary body (for example, during debate on the floor), members' roles are often highly colored by their committee memberships and standing. The next circle comprises what could be called direct congressional staff: individuals who work either for a member of Congress or for a committee or subcommittee. The third circle consists of four support agencies, which can be considered indirect congressional staff. The support agencies are used by the Congress as a means of acquiring information that direct staffs would find hard or impossible to obtain. The support agencies vary in their degree of autonomy from the Congress and sometimes serve others outside the Congress.

Direct Congressional Staff. Direct staff consist of those who work directly for a member (personal staff) and those who work for a committee or subcommittee (committee staff). Their functions are different, although there is some overlap, and exceptions are common.

Personal staff have two general responsibilities: constituent casework and legislative assistance. Casework entails all manner of help for constituents and liaison between them and their representative: answering mail, investigating specific problems involving the federal government (for example, a Social Security check that fails to arrive), meeting with constituents or interest groups, and so on. Legislative assistance is focused on the legislative process; it includes such activities as gathering information, obtaining valuable intelligence about other members' concerns or likely votes, and drafting legislation.

The number of personal staff who work for a member is influenced by several factors. In 1978, the typical Representative had fifteen staff members, but the actual number varied with the members' preferences and allocation of staff budget. Senators, who generally represent more constituents, had an average of thirty-five staff in 1978. The range in the Senate is very large, however, because Senators' staff budgets vary with the population of the state that they represent.

Committee staff work centers almost entirely on legislative affairs. Typically, they are under the control of either the committee or subcommittee chair or the ranking minority member, but, to varying degrees, they also provide support to other committee members. Accordingly, a member has access not only to personal staff but also to staff working for each of the several committees and subcommittees of which he or she is a member.

Because of the differing responsibilities of personal and committee staff, substantive experts more frequently work for committees. Exceptions are common, however, and many members have experts, including doctoral-level scientists, on their personal staffs, either as interns or as permanent staff.

Support Agencies. Members of Congress obtain information not only from their own staffs but also from the staffs of four congressional support agencies: the Congressional Research Service, the Congressional Budget Office, the General Accounting Office, and the Office of Technology Assessment. The information about research that these agencies provide to the Congress—including evaluative information—includes independently conducted research, various types of critical synthesis and secondary analysis, and straightforward reporting of the research literature.

Although the functions and products of the four support agencies overlap considerably, they differ in ways that determine how Congress makes use of them. Perhaps the most critical difference for readers of this sourcebook is that they tend to use substantially different methods in investigating issues. As a result, it is not uncommon for two or more support agencies to investigate the same problem, in some instances at the request of the same committee. Efforts are made to coordinate investigations and avoid excessive overlap, but each agency works largely independently of the others.

The Congressional Research Service (CRS) is a part of the Library of Congress and is the oldest and perhaps the most frequently used congressional support agency. The function of CRS is to perform library research for members of Congress and to provide access to sources of information. It has a staff of 700, but it also uses the services of other Library of Congress units. In response to frequently asked questions, CRS publishes "issue briefs" summarizing literature on the topic. In other cases, information is provided directly to the requester—in a form as brief as a telephone call or as extensive as a twenty- to thirty-page paper. Evaluative research is often cited in response to requests, and, at one point, CRS developed a review of the conduct of evaluation research for a Senate committee.

The General Accounting Office (GAO) is by far the largest support agency. It has a staff of almost 5,000. It is headed by the Comptroller General, an appointee of the President (confirmed by the Senate) who serves a fifteen-year term. GAO's principal evaluation function is to conduct program audits. In contrast to the work of the CRS and other congressional support agencies, most GAO studies involve actual fieldwork. The studies are based on an accounting or auditing model and emphasize how well public funds have been used. Many of these evaluations are probably best characterized as management reviews; typically, they describe problems and inefficiencies in program management and make specific recommendations for improvements.

In recent years, however, GAO has developed a second evaluation function. The Congressional Budget and Impoundment Control Act of 1974 authorized GAO to "review and evaluate the results of government programs and activities carried on under existing law." To carry out these functions, the GAO established a separate branch, the Institute for Program Evaluation (IPE). Its goal is to carry out program evaluations and make its own and other evaluations available to Congress.

A third, far smaller support agency is the Congressional Budget Office (CBO), which was also created by the Congressional Budget and Impoundment Control Act of 1974. Much of CBO's staff of about 200 is devoted to functions required by the current role of the Congress in designing the budget: estimating the costs (and savings) resulting from pending legislation, macroeconomic forecasting (essential for estimating federal revenues and the costs of many programs, such as unemployment insurance), and scorekeeping (tracking federal expenditures on a continuing basis). About a third of the agency's staff, however, produces policy analyses pertinent to legislative concerns. These analyses investigate both the situation that engendered concern and the probable effects of possible legislative responses. These analyses frequently draw on evaluation research, often linking it to economic information and analysis. In some cases, CBO conducts its own evaluation research as part of a policy analysis, but it lacks the capacity to generate independent data. The fourth support agency is the Office of Technology Assessment (OTA). OTA was created in 1972 to assist Congress in assessing the implications of technology, broadly defined as the application of scientific principles. It differs somewhat in its operations from the other support agencies. Because OTA's role is to synthesize current scientific knowledge about particular problems, it is organized into substantive research groups, each advised by an outside panel of scientists. Its full-time staff of 135 is relatively small, and it relies on consultants, some of whom serve in-house for specific periods, and others of whom are employed on an ad hoc basis when needed. In many respects, technology assessment is similar to evaluation research, except that its focus is a general problem rather than a specific program. In addition, technology assessment is often broader, encompassing technical, social, and economic variables.

Although only GAO includes a formal organizational entity whose primary function is evaluation research, all the support agencies are instrumental—in various ways and to varying degrees—in providing the Congress with evaluative information. Moreover, from the perspective of the Congress, the role of the four support agencies in transmitting, evaluating, and synthesizing evaluation research conducted by executive agencies and others is at least as important as their role in performing independent evaluations.

The Present Volume

Each of the chapters in this volume discusses the role of evaluation in congressional deliberations on one or more topics during the 96th Congress. The chapters focus not only on how evaluations were used (or misused or ignored) but also on the potential role of evaluation in the legislative process. The chapters differ from each other for several reasons: the different congressional positions and responsibilities of the authors, their varying backgrounds, and the idiosyncratic characteristics of the issues, key members, and committees in each case. The first chapter is by Scott Brown, who served as a Fellow through the direct sponsorship of AAAS. During his fellowship, he was a legislative assistant for the Senate Subcommittee on Housing and Urban Affairs. His responsibilities included legislative tasks, such as preparing briefing materials and drafting committee reports, as well as drafting legislation. Brown has a doctorate in environmental psychology.

Brown's chapter concerns legislative deliberations about requirements for public transportation systems to provide access for handicapped persons. His focus is on how evaluations, developed both inside and outside the Congress, yielded radically different conclusions about the reasonableness of various strategies for mandating access for the handicapped. His chapter deals both with the misuse of information and with the structure of the information that was used by Congress. He draws a number of lessons from this experience about how evaluators and policy analysts can better make their data and conclusions available to Congress.

The second chapter was written by Daniel Koretz, a coeditor of this volume. Koretz served as a policy analyst with the Congressional Budget Office during his fellowship year (sponsored by the American Psychological Association), and he has remained in that role to the present. He has a Ph.D. in developmental psychology and specializes in research methods and program evaluation. His primary responsibilities at CBO have been in the areas of health and education.

Koretz's experience in Congress is more extensive than that of the other authors, and his chapter is the most didactic effort to explain how evaluators can aim their work toward the congressional audience. As an example of congressional use of evaluation research, he uses his work for the CBO on Professional Standards Review Organizations (PSROs). His conclusions address ways in which evaluation research can be made understandable and useful to intelligent and interested policy makers, both in the Congress and elsewhere.

Pamela Doty, author of the third chapter, served in the Office of Technology Assessment as a Congressional Fellow within the health program. She holds a Ph.D. in sociology, and her prior research dealt with the structure of health-care services. At OTA, she was involved in several projects, including one that dealt with the supply of physicians.

Doty's chapter draws on her experiences in developing two assessments for OTA to analyze the role that OTA plays as a research broker. She focuses on the translation of scientific research, such as evaluation, on behalf of Congress and on the interrelations of methodological and political concerns.

The fourth chapter was contributed by Leonard Saxe, a coeditor of this volume. His chapter is based on work done at OTA, where he served as a Fellow (sponsored by OTA). Saxe has a Ph.D. in social psychology, and his research has concerned the conduct of experiments in applied settings. At OTA, his principal responsibility was to direct a project on the cost-effectiveness of medical technology.

Saxe's chapter concerns efforts to assess the efficacy and cost-effectiveness of psychotherapy. Like several of the other chapters, it is a case study of a legislative problem that required evaluative data, although it focuses on the development of research evidence, not on the legislative discussions. He describes how interest in evaluation by members of Congress led to a particular proposal to incorporate evaluation data in future policy decisions and the resistance that this proposal incurred.

Final Notes

It should be clear from these brief descriptions that the chapters of this volume do not systematically represent Congress's interest in and use of evaluation research. Although the authors worked in very different settings, three of the four were trained in psychology. Moreover, several congressional perspectives on evaluation (for example, the perspective of GAO) are not represented at all. Further, the focus of the chapters is almost entirely on the use of evaluation, not on the development of evaluation research as a potential tool for congressional decision making. It should not be necessary to note that evaluation developed to meet legislative purposes would almost certainly take a different form.

Nonetheless, these chapters should be of interest—and use—to many evaluators. They provide a first-hand look, from the perspective of researchers, into congressional use of evaluation. Despite their diversity, they are surprisingly consistent in describing some basic patterns in congressional use of evaluation and in suggesting ways of improving that use. Moreover, many of the generalizations that appear in this volume are applicable, to varying degrees, to other policymaking contexts as well.

Acknowledgements

Above all, the editors and authors are indebted to those who made their experiences in the Congress possible: the American Association for the Advancement of Science, which developed and which coordinates the Congressional Science Fellowship program; the professional societies and congressional support agencies that sponsored their fellowships; and the members, committees, support agencies, and staffs that were their hosts during their fellowship years.

Leonard Saxe
Daniel Koretz
Editors

8

References

Aherback, J. D. "Changes in Congressional Oversight." In C. H. Weiss and H. Barton (Eds.), *Making Bureaucracies Work.* Beverly Hills, Calif.: Sage, 1979.

Fox, H. W., and Hammond, S. W. *Congressional Staffs: The Invisible Force in American Lawmaking.* New York: Free Press, 1977.

Leonard Saxe, assistant professor of psychology at Boston University, is a social psychologist whose research concerns the conduct of experiments in applied settings. He is currently teaching at the University of Haifa in Israel on a Fulbright fellowship.

Daniel Koretz is a policy analyst with the Congressional Budget Office, United States Congress, where he has worked in the areas of health and education. He is a developmental psychologist who specializes in program evaluation and research methods.

For research studies to have an impact on the
development of legislation, the information must
fit the legislative context, be in a form that is
usable by congressional decision makers, and
address the pivotal issues on which congressional
deliberations have settled.

A Case Study of Evaluation
Research in the Legislative
Process: Public Transportation
for the Handicapped

Scott D. Brown

The product of evaluation research and the other forms of policy research is information. The consumers of policy research have widely
differing needs for policy-related data, depending on their role in the
decision-making process.

The executive branch of government, which is charged with
the implementation of public law, is most concerned with identifying the most efficient means for achieving the goals expressed by legislation. Federal, state, and local governments are frequent consumers
of both summative and formative program evaluation research, as
well as of policy analysis and cost-benefit analysis.

In judicial proceedings, litigants often use studies of various
sorts to demonstrate that the substantive or procedural requirements
of law have been met or violated. To ensure compliance with a judicial remedy, a follow-up evaluation is sometimes stipulated.

Legislators in the U.S. Congress are among the most diversified
consumers of policy and evaluative research. Evaluation studies, pol-

L. Saxe, D. Koretz (Eds.). *New Directions for Program Evaluation: Making Evaluation
Research Useful to Congress,* no. 14. San Francisco: Jossey-Bass, June 1982.

icy analyses, and related reports can all be used in the development of legislative proposals. Legislators have staffs whose responsibility is to collect and synthesize such information. In addition, various agencies support the work of legislators. Evaluative research is used in the formulation of new legislation, in congressional review of administrative regulations (Brown and Cahn, 1980), and through oversight of existing programs.

The purpose of this chapter is to examine the role that evaluation and policy research plays in the legislative process. For research studies to have an impact on the development of legislation, the information must fit the legislative context, be in a form that is usable by congressional decision makers, and address the pivotal issues on which congressional deliberations have settled.

To illustrate how Congress uses social research, the controversy over the Department of Transportation's (DOT) regulations to implement the handicapped accessibility provisions set forth in Section 504 of the Rehabilitation Act of 1973 is examined in detail. This case study examines the legislation, the political context, policy studies that were used, and the course of events that ultimately led to the demise of a $25 billion bill that had been passed in various forms by both Houses of Congress. Within the context of the legislative process, the relative impact of empirical evidence about program impacts is examined. The issues that affected how and why certain studies had an effect on the legislative process are discussed. These issues have implications for evaluators seeking to have an impact on the legislative process.

Case Study: Public Transportation for the Handicapped

In 1970 the Urban Mass Transportation Act (UMTA) was amended to require that localities make "special efforts" to provide transportation for elderly and handicapped persons. Section 504 of the Rehabilitation Act of 1973 required that all federally supported services be accessible to the handicapped (Public Law 93-112). In response to this mandate, federal assistance to state and local governments from UMTA funds was made contingent on the provision of accessible transportation services for handicapped persons. Nevertheless, many localities failed to develop plans or implement services to meet the transportation needs of the handicapped.

In response to what was perceived as inordinate delay on the part of state and local government, the Department of Transportation issued regulations stipulating in detail the types and levels of transportation services to be provided for handicapped persons as necessary conditions for the receipt of mass transportation assistance and, potentially, all assistance from the federal government.

The DOT regulations, which became effective on July 2, 1979, specified that new buses acquired after the effective date of the regulation must be accessible to handicapped persons; within ten years, one half of all peak hour bus service must be accessible to handicapped persons; within thirty years, key rail transit stations (about 40 percent of all rail stations) must be accessible to the handicapped, while inaccessible rail stations must have connecting bus service to accessible stations; waivers of the requirements could be provided if the locality, in consultation with the handicapped community, could establish that "alternate service substantially as good or better than" the service mandated in the regulations was being provided; and from the third year after the effective date of the regulation, until program accessibility is achieved, "interim accessible service" must be provided (*Federal Register,* 1979, p. 31442).

Political Context. In the spring of 1980, the Carter administration sent legislation to Congress extending and expanding the authorization for federal assistance in the area of public transportation (H.R. 6890, H.R. 6964, S. 2479). The legislation itself contained no measures related to accessibility for the handicapped. However, once the omnibus legislative package was introduced, it became a vehicle for a number of initiatives substantially restructuring the federal requirements for handicapped accessibility.

The UMTA legislation, which authorized expenditures of about $25 billion, was introduced at a time when the public was viewing inflation as the primary national problem and government spending as a chief cause of inflation. Partially in reaction to the federal government's handling of the economy, the November 1980 elections led to defeat of the incumbent President, a substantial reduction in Democratic membership in the House, and a Republican takeover in the Senate. It was left to a lame duck Senate and administration to push the UMTA bills through in the waning days of the 96th Congress.

Competing Studies. During consideration of the UMTA bills, a number of analyses of the likely costs and benefits of the DOT Section 504 regulations were circulated in Congress. The first study, published by the Congressional Budget Office in November 1979, was highly critical of the DOT regulations. The CBO report aroused a good deal of reaction from the press and Congress for its conclusions that the program would cost $6.8 billion during the next thirty years; enactment of the DOT regulations would benefit no more than 7 percent of all severely disabled persons; and, under the DOT approach, the cost of providing accessible transportation to disabled persons would average $38 per ride, in contrast to trips by the general public, which, on the average, cost about 85¢ (Congressional Budget Office, 1979).

In the spring of 1980, the American Coalition of Citizens with Disabilities (ACCD) sponsored a study of the DOT accessibility regulations (Cannon and Rainbow, 1980). The result was a point-by-point rebuttal of the CBO study. The ACCD report also evaluated the history of federal efforts to make public transportation accessible to the handicapped and concluded that the local option approach, in which localities are left to design accessibility programs of their own, does not work. The ACCD report also raised the civil rights issue associated with the DOT regulations and asserted that any service other than fixed-rate accessibility would constitute at most a "separate but equal" policy toward the handicapped.

The Department of Transportation issued its own evaluation study in June 1980, which also was highly critical of the CBO report (U.S. Department of Transportation, 1980). DOT tried to show that the costs associated with making bus and rail transit accessible were less than half of the CBO estimate and that the cost per trip by handicapped persons was less than a quarter of the CBO estimate.

All three reports based cost and ridership estimates on a host of assumptions. The CBO report compared the DOT approach with two other program options. One option involved purchasing a specially equipped automobile for every transportation handicapped person wishing to have one; the other option provided dial-a-ride, door-to-door van service. Because the DOT approach involved a major fixed cost associated with making bus and rail services accessible and because the dial-a-ride option had relatively low fixed costs, low estimates of ridership tended to inflate the cost per ride associated with the DOT approach when it was compared with the dial-a-ride approach. Alternately, because dial-a-ride does not benefit from economies of scale associated with fixed-route accessible services, such as those advocated by DOT, high estimates of handicapped ridership made the DOT approach more cost-effective than dial-a-ride.

Table 1 illustrates the wide differences in cost estimates between the DOT and CBO analyses. To explain how CBO arrived at a figure of nearly $4.8 billion for making bus services accessible and DOT arrived at a figure of only $1.8 billion requires us to examine assumptions that went into these analyses.

The difference in lift maintenance cost estimates is due to CBO's use of data from the Bi–State Development Corporation in St. Louis—the first metropolitan area to implement wheelchair accessible lift service on buses on a wide scale. DOT's lower maintenance estimates were based on the assumption that lifts have improved and

Table 1. Comparison of DOT and CBO Estimates of Costs
Associated with Implementation of DOT Accessibility
Regulations for Buses

	CBO (Millions)	DOT (Millions)
Lifts		
Capital	$1,380	$1,300
Maintenance	1,200	465
Fleet Expansion		
Maintenance Float	334	33
Lost Seating Capacity	1,782	0
Kneeling Feature on All Buses	78	0
Total Cost	$4,784	$1,798

Note: Excerpted from U.S. Department of Transportation (1980), p. 3.

that the resulting maintenance costs would be much lower than those experienced in St. Louis. In this case, CBO relied on available empirical data. DOT, however, relied on likely improvements in technology in reducing its estimates for maintenance costs. In default of an up-to-date assessment of maintenance costs of lift operations, either the CBO or the DOT estimate could be seen as reasonable.

Because CBO estimated that a large number of buses with lifts would be out of service for maintenance, it required a 2 percent increase in the total bus fleet to compensate for down time. In contrast, DOT assumed that some increase in the maintenance float would be necessary during the first years, but no permanent additions would have to be made. The result was a $301 million difference in fleet expansion cost estimates.

CBO estimated that the total number of buses would have to be expanded by 1.5 percent to compensate for seating capacity lost due to the provision of space on buses for wheelchairs. This aspect of fleet expansion was estimated to cost $1.782 billion. DOT, in contrast, assumed that accessibility would result in no significant loss in passenger-carrying capability. Because buses are rarely full except during rush hour and because the wheelchair space on accessible buses provides increased standing room capacity during rush hour, DOT thought this assumption was justified. Thus, the DOT cost estimate makes no provision for lost seating capacity.

CBO included $78 million in its cost estimates for providing all new buses with a special device that lowers the front steps of buses to allow easier access by blind, elderly, or other persons who have difficulty negotiating steps. DOT did not include the cost of this so-called kneeling feature in its estimate because the feature was not required by the regulations.

The resulting cost differences associated with bringing bus service into compliance with the DOT regulations differ by three billion dollars. The two reports showed similar disparities over costs associated with bringing rail service into compliance with the DOT regulations.

To further exacerbate differences in evaluations of cost, the DOT estimate of the number of handicapped persons who would benefit from the DOT accessibility program was twice that of the CBO estimate. Surprisingly, both the DOT and CBO estimates were based on the same analysis of the travel preferences of handicapped persons (U.S. Department of Transportation, 1978a). The DOT-sponsored study indicated that there were about 13.4 million transportation handicapped persons living in the United States (U.S. Department of Transportation, 1976). About 7.4 million handicapped persons live in cities served by public transportation (U.S. Department of Transportation, 1978b). About 4.9 million transportation handicapped persons living in areas served by public transit lived within one-half mile of a bus stop.

The 1978 survey of 1,500 transportation handicapped persons living within one-half mile of a bus stop indicated that slightly fewer than 60 percent believed that they would use public transit if it was accessible. The survey suggested that about 3 million transportation handicapped persons living within one-half mile of a bus stop would respond similarly. However, because of the likelihood of noncommitment survey bias (the tendency of survey respondents to respond to interview or questionnaire items in a more socially desirable way than they otherwise would if some actual personal commitment was associated with the response), survey respondents who reported barriers between their residence and a bus stop (for example, curbs, no sidewalks, major intersections) were excluded from the estimate of the number of handicapped persons who actually would use accessible public transit. The adjusted estimate of the number of persons likely to benefit from accessible transit, 1.4 million, was adopted by DOT in its estimates of ridership resulting from implementation of the proposed regulations.

The DOT estimate of likely handicapped ridership was criticized in the ACCD report as being too low. The barriers to effective use of accessible transit included "surly drivers" and "inconvenient schedules." The ACCD report concluded that the likely impact of these and many other so-called barriers would be far less than that calculated in the DOT survey. The ACCD also noted the likelihood that, as handicapped persons develop more skills, and as employment among handicapped persons increases, demand for public transportation among handicapped persons will be much higher than that implied by the DOT study. In contrast, CBO cut the DOT estimates of handicapped ridership in half. This reduction, to about 750,000 persons, was based on studies of handicapped ridership in cities that offered accessible bus service.

Both DOT and the ACCD criticized the CBO conclusion, because most of the studies on which it was based were studies of pilot programs with severe service and eligibility restrictions. Moreover, many of these programs had been in existence for a relatively short period, and implementation problems and lack of consumer awareness may have acted to reduce ridership.

In summary, the CBO, ACCD, and DOT reports provide three very different sets of conclusions about the costs and benefits of implementation of DOT accessibility regulations. Each report has merit, and the assumptions that each used were all based on careful analysis of existing studies and other information. In the context of congressional deliberations on federal assistance for mass transit, the CBO report was used to support assertions that the DOT regulations were unreasonably expensive and that they would do relatively little to meet the travel needs of transportation handicapped persons. The ACCD and DOT reports were used in defense of the DOT regulations.

The Course of Events. On July 1, 1979, the DOT handicapped accessibility regulations were implemented after a long public review process in which handicapped groups, localities, and public transit operators provided extensive input. The national handicapped groups, including the American Coalition of Citizens with Disabilities, the Easter Seals Society, the National Rehabilitation Association, and the American Council of the Blind all supported the final version of the regulations. Opposition to the regulations came from a number of local governments, some local handicapped groups who feared a loss of dial-a-ride services, and the American Public Transit Association (APTA). APTA brought suit against the Department of Transportation, asserting that the DOT regulations were arbitrary and capricious. In the initial suit, the DOT regulations were upheld (*American Public Transit Association* v. *Lewis,* 1981).

In November 1979, CBO issued its report on the costs of implementing the DOT regulations. A number of newspaper editorials cited the regulations as an example of government waste (for example, "Hindsight on Helping the Handicapped," 1980). On February 19, 1980, the DOT issued its response to the CBO report.

In late winter, the Carter administration sent to Congress a number of legislative proposals amending the UMTA. The Senate

Subcommittee on Housing and Urban Affairs, which is responsible for urban mass transit legislation, held hearings on the UMTA legislation early in March 1980. DOT Secretary Neil Goldschmidt was asked only one question regarding the progress of implementation of the DOT accessibility regulations. Otherwise, no mention was made of the regulations by Housing subcommittee members or witnesses. Despite the recent court action of APTA to halt implementation of the regulations, APTA representatives made no mention of the regulations. The failure of APTA to raise the issue may have been due to the fact that, at that time, even APTA had not seized on the UMTA legislation as a vehicle for amending the DOT accessibility regulations.

UMTA hearings were held by the House Subcommittee on Surface Transportation on March 26. By that time, the situation had changed substantially. Representative James Cleveland of New Hampshire had circulated a letter to members of the House and Senate that used cost and ridership statistics from the CBO report to attack the DOT accessibility regulations.

During the hearings, Representative Cleveland questioned Secretary Goldschmidt about the House oversight report and the feasibility of the DOT accessibility regulations. Secretary Goldschmidt's response appeared to indicate both his surprise at being questioned about the issue and his lukewarm support for the regulations:

> Was that question for me? Is anybody willing to step up here and answer it? . . . As a mayor, Congressman, I supported that position [the local option approach to accessibility]. As a cochairman of the U.S. Conference of Mayors' Committee on Transportation, I supported that position. I am not sure, however, that this is an appropriate position for our Department to take at this time (U.S. Senate, Subcommittee on Surface Transportation, 1980, p. 71).

The local option position advocated by Representative Cleveland basically left it up to localities to develop a program of accessible transportation that complied with the mandate of Section 504. DOT would monitor compliance with section 504, and it could cut off transportation assistance funds if a locality was found to be offering inadequate services.

In contrast to the Senate hearings, the House Testimony of APTA and the National League of Cities criticized the DOT regulations and favored the local option approach. Moreover, one handicapped group, Overcoming Mobility Barriers International Incorporated, was represented at the House hearings. This group opposed the DOT regulations on the grounds that the regulations were inefficient and that they would act to deprive handicapped persons of demand responsive services that they were already receiving. The presence of a single, rather obscure handicapped group that opposed the regulations and the absence of all the major handicapped groups suggests not all sides of the issue were aired at the hearing.

At this point in the process, the press, a House oversight subcommittee, and even a handicapped group had come out in opposition to the DOT accessibility regulations on grounds of cost. Neither DOT nor the major handicapped groups that favored the DOT regulations had mobilized an effective lobbying and public information campaign.

Despite DOT's prompt rebuttal to the CBO report, Secretary Goldschmidt appears to have been surprised by the questions about the Section 504 regulations during the House reauthorization hearings. Not until the summer of 1980 did the American Coalition of Citizens with Disabilities begin to circulate a draft rebuttal to the CBO study. DOT's failure to press its case for implementation of the existing Section 504 regulations and ACCD's delay in preparing its rebuttal left the CBO report as the major analysis of costs associated with implementation of Section 504 regulations.

In the Senate, the UMTA legislation was marked up and reported out of the Senate Subcommittee on Housing and Urban Affairs on May 15, 1980 (U.S. Senate Subcommittee on Housing and Urban Affairs, 1980). The Subcommittee passed no amendments relating to the DOT regulations and included no language pertaining to the subject. Additional views of Senators Jake Garn of Utah and William Armstrong of Colorado, however, did raise the key issue on which events ultimately would turn in the Senate: "We believe that inflation is the overwhelming domestic problem facing this country today and that it will continue to devastate the economy until such time as spending by the federal government is reduced significantly" (U.S. Senate, Subcommittee on Housing and Urban Affairs, 1980, p. 26).

In its markup, the House Committee on Public Works and Transportation included Representative Cleveland's amendment to institute a local option whereby states could submit accessibility plans to DOT for approval and obtain a waiver of the requirements set forth in the DOT regulations. The amendment included a variety of requirements relating to the cost and availability of services and to consultation with the handicapped community. In sum, substantially fewer services were required under the Cleveland amendment than under the DOT regulations. No fixed rail accessibility for existing stations was required. During the first two years of the program, transportation services to handicapped persons were required to be provided within twenty-four hours of a request, and accessible buses were not mandated.

By the time the UMTA bill reached the floor of the Senate in June 1980, forces in favor of local option had found advocates in Senators James Exon and Edward Zorinsky of Nebraska. Senators Exon and Zorinsky sought to introduce the Cleveland local option amendment as a floor amendment to the Senate version of the UMTA bill. The staff of Senator Harrison Williams of New Jersey, the manager of the bill, worked with the Zorinsky staff to develop a compromise measure that would be acceptable to both sides of the Senate. This measure was passed by consent. The full bill was passed by the Senate and sent to the House for consideration.

House action on the UMTA bill did not occur until December, the last month of the 96th Congress. Congressman James Howard of New Jersey, Chairman of the Public Works and Transportation Committee, managed the bill on the floor of the House. To expedite passage of the UMTA bill, Howard introduced a floor amendment replacing the Section 223 language passed in the House markup with language that closely approximated the Williams-Zorinsky language used in the Senate version.

Congressman Cleveland found the Howard language unacceptable, and he introduced a substitute amendment similar to that adopted during markup. The substitute amendment would have further reduced requirements for demand-responsive service for the handicapped and eliminated language relating to comparability of trip time between accessible and nonaccessible services. The measure raised response time for accessible service to twenty-four hours from the time of a request and included language giving priority to medically related trips.

The controversy generated by the Howard and Cleveland amendments opened the floor of the House to debate on the costs of the Section 504 regulations. The debates included frequent reference to the CBO evaluation of the costs and benefits of the DOT approach. However, since the majority leadership in both the House and the Senate had already adopted measures offering localities the option to avoid many of the requirements of the DOT regulations, the impact of the CBO report had already been felt; further reference to the CBO analysis was used to support the extensive cuts advocated by Cleveland.

At only two points in the debates was the CBO study directly criticized. Congressmen George Miller of California and Paul Simon of Illinois, using arguments developed by the ACCD, criticized CBO's cost and ridership estimates. However, they argued not in support of the DOT regulations but to prevent the further reductions proposed in the Cleveland amendment.

The DOT analyses of cost and ridership were never used in these debates. There appears to have been a good deal of consensus that DOT "bureaucrats" had gone too far on the accessibility issue in Section 504. Reference to DOT's analysis of costs and benefits would have only stirred up more furor over governmental waste.

One important theme in these debates was the effects of the November elections, which seemed to indicate strong national support for cutting back on federal programs. Although the Democrats retained control of the House, there was concern that, if the accessibility requirements were not substantially reduced, the entire UMTA bill would not pass the Senate as the result of a Republican filibuster.

Other key issues in the debate over the Cleveland substitute amendment were the support of handicapped groups for the full DOT measures, the questionable effectiveness of the Cleveland measure in providing a basic level of service for handicapped persons, and the fact that the Howard measure was an obvious compromise that took a wide spectrum of interests on the issue into account. Nevertheless, the Cleveland amendment failed by only two votes in a recorded vote, and this set the stage for Cleveland to take another run at the Howard provision.

When floor action on the UMTA bill resumed two days later, Cleveland introduced an amendment, worked out with Congressman Howard, that eliminated the comparability clause, which required accessible trips to have response times roughly comparable to those of regular service. The amendment also eliminated provisions under which handicapped persons could bring suit in case of noncompliance, and it included requirements for extensive congressional oversight.

Arguments on behalf of this amendment centered on assuring passage of the bill in the Senate and on further reducing restrictions on local governments. The arguments against the amendment were similar to those presented two days earlier, but they did not have the same effect. The Cleveland compromise measure was passed and sent to the Senate.

The Senate took final action on the House-passed version of the UMTA bill on the second to last day of the 96th Congress. Republican opposition to the accessibility measures was overshadowed by their opposition to the passage of a $25 billion bill immediately prior to the beginning of a new Congress, in which the Republicans would control the Senate and a Republican President, intent on reducing federal spending, would take office. In the waning hours of the 96th Congress, the Republicans filibustered the UMTA bill, and the measure died. This left the DOT accessibility regulations in place.

Discussion

The CBO evaluation report had considerably more impact in persuading Congress that the DOT regulations were inefficient than either the ACCD or DOT cost-benefit analyses. The CBO numbers were cited frequently and only rarely disputed. Given the willingness of congressional leadership on both sides of the aisle to support changes in the accessibility requirements, the ACCD and DOT arguments appeared to have had little effect.

The CBO study served to focus congressional attention on the DOT accessibility regulations. In an environment of cost consciousness, there was substantial political pressure to follow up on the CBO recommendations with measures that cut back on the accessibility provisions.

The ACCD and DOT reports faced an insurmountable burden of proof in contesting the CBO study. The CBO report was the first on the scene, and, despite some questionable analysis, it made a number of very strong assertions about the high costs of the DOT accessibility program. The ACCD and DOT analyses were placed on the defensive by the CBO study. Rather than focusing on the merits of the program, they were forced to explain why the CBO analysis was wrong.

As a congressional support agency, CBO wore the mantle of impartiality (see the chapter by Koretz in this volume). Congress relies on numbers provided by CBO in assessing the fiscal impact of federal programs. If CBO says that the DOT accessibility program will cost $6.8 billion, then most members of Congress are likely to think that it will cost $6.8 billion. DOT, in contrast, was the target of considerable criticism from members of Congress. Given the pervasive public sentiment against "big government," if the DOT report had been used in the debates, the public would have viewed it as a case of bureaucrats' attempting to defend expensive programs that guaranteed their own jobs. The ACCD suffered from being partisan as well. Irrespective of the quality of the analysis, the fact that ACCD represented a special—and somewhat narrow—interest was lost on no one.

The DOT regulations might have fared better in Congress if the White House and the Department of Transportation had mobilized a more active lobbying effort. In many respects, DOT appears to have been caught off guard by the Cleveland amendments. Once the battle had been joined, it was not completely clear that DOT was willing to fight for the regulations. If this was the case, it may have been due to concern that major opposition to reductions in the accessibility program would jeopardize the passage of the entire bill.

The public sentiment that influenced movements to cut back on the DOT accessibility program was felt in the November election. In response to what was viewed as a national mandate to reduce federal spending, Senate Republicans ignored the accessibility program and went after the entire UMTA authorization bill. They successfully filibustered the bill, leaving it up to the Reagan administration to consider the merits of sending up a $25 billion mass transit package. This left the accessibility program untouched. APTA continued to press its civil suit against the program, and, after a change in administration, it found the defendant to be considerably less enthusiastic in its defense of the Section 504 regulations. Not surprisingly, APTA won, and the DOT regulations were returned to the federal bureaucracy for substantial revision.

Implications for Policy Scientists

Evaluators and policy scientists who wish to increase the impact of their work on congressional deliberations will benefit from a number of considerations raised by the case of the DOT accessibility regulations.

Source. Because members of Congress and their staffs generally lack the expertise to evaluate the quality of the statistics and the analyses that they receive, the source of the studies is used to answer questions about the quality of the analysis. The more politically disinterested the source, the more likely that its numbers will be accepted by Congress. The congressional support agencies have high credibility with Congress. The reports prepared by special interest groups are viewed as least reliable. Because federal agencies and the White House often have a stake in the success of a particular piece of legislation, analyses from the executive branch are treated more as special-interest reports than as impartial analyses.

Congressional Dissemination. Just as important as preparing a credible report is getting it in front of people who can do something with it. The congressional support agencies, unless work is being done by special request, automatically disseminate their reports to all potentially interested congressional offices.

Ensuring that the report gets read can require some selling. Hearings provide one useful forum for presenting data, but one's work must be known for this to happen. Meetings with individual staff ensure that there will be someone in a Congressman's office who is knowledgeable on the study. The one-to-one process is also important in cultivating support on the Hill. Although Congressmen Miller and Simon used some of the ACCD arguments in debate, they did not provide much help in making other Congressmen aware of the study. In contrast, Congressman Cleveland sent a "Dear Colleague" letter publicizing the CBO findings.

Where the direct approach does not succeed, working through the press often will, especially if the findings are of a certain kind. The press seems to be the most interested in research that points to government error and waste. Still, with a little work, it may be possible to get press coverage for promising programs, programmatic happy endings, or studies documenting substantial unmet needs for particular goods or services. The only caveat here is that care must be taken to assure that study results are not misinterpreted or otherwise misused by the press.

Conclusiveness. Congressional staff rarely have extensive training in policy analysis and research. As Koretz notes in his chapter, lengthy discussions of sampling error or sensitivity analysis will go unread. The most important part of any report that is sent to Congress is the executive summary. It must be brief and clear. If the conclusions of the study are not stated, plainly and simply, at the very beginning, they will never be seen. All the information in the CBO report that was cited in debates on the House and Senate floor can be found in the executive summary of that report.

Timeliness. For a policy study to have any use for congressional staff, it must reach them well in advance of the time when the issue is considered on the floor of the House and Senate. By the time the ACCD report was published, the House had already included the local option amendment in the UMTA bill. There was considerable momentum in both houses of Congress to revise the Section 504 regulations. The press was full of articles and editorials citing the CBO cost estimates long before DOT or ACCD published their rebuttal analyses. To the extent that opinions about the costs of the Section 504 regulations already had been shaped, the DOT and ACCD reports had little impact on the legislative process.

Interpretation of the Numbers. The impact of a policy study depends on the extent to which the report coincides with key themes in Congress. The CBO study focused on what it would cost the federal government to provide accessible mass transit under a variety of options. The ACCD report addressed the cost issues, but it also discussed the civil rights implications of accessibility, the likely improvements that accessible transit would make in the quality of life of handicapped people, and other qualitative issues. It failed to highlight what the DOT accessibility program would cost to the government under its analysis.

At the time of the deliberations on UMTA, money was the key theme in Congress. By not focusing on the money issue, the ACCD report sacrificed impact that it could have had. The ACCD report was a very adequate rebuttal of many of the CBO arguments, but it never summarized its findings in such a way as to counter the CBO numbers. The DOT report did do this, but because of the low esteem in which most Congressmen then held the federal government, pushing the DOT report before Congress could possibly have done more harm than good.

If an evaluator who works in a policy context is going to go to the trouble to conduct a good study, and if someone is willing to pay the cost, it makes good sense to structure the work so that the relevant decision makers can benefit from it. This is not to say that social scientists should be advocates, although many are. Effective dissemination of policy-relevant research to Congress is a beneficial end in itself. As members of Congress become better informed of the true impacts of legislative options, they will be able to make better decisions.

References

American Public Transit Association v. *Lewis,* 485 F. Supp 811 (D.D.C. 1980) *reversed on appeal,* No. 80-1497 (D.C. Cir., May 26, 1981).

Brown, S., and Cahn, J. "The Legislative Veto: Congress Evaluates the Federal Regulatory Process." Paper presented at the annual meeting of the Evaluation Network, Memphis, Tenn., September 1980.

Cannon, D., and Rainbow, F. *Full Mobility: Counting the Costs of the Alternatives.* Washington, D.C.: American Coalition of Citizens with Disabilities, 1980.

Congressional Budget Office. *Urban Transportation for Handicapped Persons: Alternative Federal Approaches.* Washington, D.C.: U.S. Government Printing Office, 1979.

Federal Register, 44 (106), May 31, 1979.

"Hindsight on Helping the Handicapped." *New York Times,* February 16, 1980.

Public Law 93-112, The Rehabilitation Act of 1973, 87, Stat. 355 (codified as 29 U.S.C. 701794).

U.S. Department of Transportation. *Transportation Problems of the Transportation Handicapped.* Washington, D.C.: U.S. Government Printing Office, 1976.

U.S. Department of Transportation. *Summary Report of Data from the National Survey of Handicapped People.* Washington, D.C.: U.S. Government Printing Office, 1978a.

U.S. Department of Transportation. *Technical Report of the National Survey of Transportation Handicapped People.* Washington, D.C.: U.S. Government Printing Office, 1978b.

U.S. Department of Transportation. "Comments on Congressional Budget Office Report on Urban Transportation for Handicapped Persons." Congressional Memorandum, 1980.

U.S. House of Representatives, Subcommittee on Surface Transportation.

Amending the Urban Mass Transportation Act. Washington, D.C.: U.S. Government Printing Office, 1981.

U.S. Senate, Subcommittee on Housing and Urban Affairs. *Federal Public Transportation Act of 1980.* Washington, D.C.: U.S. Government Printing Office, 1980.

Scott Brown spent a year on the staff of the U.S. Senate Subcommittee on Housing and Urban Affairs as a Society for Research in Child Development/American Association for the Advancement of Science Congressional Science Fellow. He is director of research for the Council of State Housing Agencies, a trade association representing state housing finance agencies.

*Institutional factors that constrain the Congress's
use of evaluation research are illustrated by a case
history of congressional deliberations about the
Professional Standards Review Organization
program, and concrete guidelines are offered
for evaluators.*

Developing Useful Evaluations:
A Case History and Some
Practical Guidelines

Daniel Koretz

The ultimate goal of most evaluation research is to affect policy, even if those who conduct the research have no plans themselves to bring their work to policy makers. Some of the characteristics that make evaluations useful to policy makers, however, are independent of the technical competence of the evaluation. Indeed, they can be diametrically opposed to the criteria of "good" research reporting imposed by the professional culture of evaluators. As a result, policy makers use evaluation research less often than they otherwise would and misinterpret it more often than need be.

This chapter focuses on one context for the use of evaluation in the formation of policy: the use of evaluation by the U.S. Congress. The chapter is organized in three sections. The first describes congressional use of evaluation in general terms. The second is a case history of the Professional Standards Review Organization (PSRO) program. The third presents guidelines for evaluators who wish to in-

The opinions discussed here are those of the author and do not necessarily reflect the official position of the Congressional Budget Office or its staff.

L. Saxe, D. Koretz (Eds.). *New Directions for Program Evaluation: Making Evaluation Research Useful to Congress*, no. 14. San Francisco: Jossey-Bass, June 1982.

crease the chances that their work will reach policy makers and be correctly understood. These guidelines should be helpful in making evaluations useful to other policy-making institutions as well, such as state and local legislatures and executive agencies at all levels of government.

How Does the Congress Use Evaluation?

The Congress is a complex institution, and its use of evaluation —or any other type of information—is accordingly both complex and highly variable. Nonetheless, several broad generalizations can be made about its use of evaluations. First, the Congress often obtains results of summative evaluations only indirectly, through the filters of executive agencies, congressional support agencies, lobbyists, and others. Second, some of these filters lack the technical expertise to decipher and assess evaluations, and others are not interested in presenting an unbiased overview of the available research. Third, for the most part, members of Congress and their staffs also lack relevant technical training. Finally, the Congress does not behave like an ideal judge or jury, focused single-mindedly on uncovering the truth. Rather, it is devoted to reconciling the competing claims of an enormous range of interests. It is unlike a jury in that all its members have a stake in the outcome of its deliberations. Not only will interests that they hold important, for principled or other reasons, win or lose as a result of their decisions, but their own positions are at stake. The "truth" (and, to the extent that it can claim to be the truth, evaluation research) plays an important part in the process, but not the only part. To restate this point in somewhat different terms, different constituents may have very different views of what makes a given program worthwhile and whether it is, or can be, successful. Evaluation results will be used, often in conflicting ways, by different and competing interests.

The researcher who contributes evaluation to the Congressional process or to other policy makers accordingly faces two hurdles. Even evaluators who have no immediate intention of contributing to the process of policy making may find it useful to work to overcome these hurdles, since their work may end up in the policy arena. The first hurdle lies in designing and presenting the research in a way that makes it comprehensible to a reasonably well-educated layperson. The second, closely related hurdle lies in expressing the results in a way that minimizes the likelihood of the work's being misinterpreted as it is recounted—and refiltered—time after time.

How Does the Congress Gain Access to Evaluation?

In situations where evaluation research is important to the Congress (for example, when a controversial program needs reauthorization to continue operating, or when a program faces proposals for structural changes or changes in funding), the Congress generally obtains it in diverse forms from a number of different channels. Accordingly, the Congress often does not receive a single, clearly authoritative statement of a program's effects. Rather, it receives a variety of possibly conflicting views, some based on different data, some based on comparable data but using different analytic methods, and so on. Moreover, since evaluation research is often interpreted and paraphrased before it reaches Congress, even a single study can be used to substantiate opposing arguments.

Six channels are particularly important: committee and personal staffs, formal hearings, the media, executive agencies, congressional support agencies, and interest groups.

Committee and Personal Staffs. Congressional staffs are undoubtedly the most important channel through which members obtain information, including evaluation results. The single most important function of many staffers is to obtain needed information for their member or committee—what Zweig (1979) called the staff's "information scanning and trading" function. Moreover, even information that comes through other channels (for example, from lobbyists) will often also pass through the channel of personal and committee staff before reaching the member. When evaluations are germane to the member's or committee's particular interests, staff will use the brief time available to obtain relevant studies and summaries wherever they can. Often, however, they obtain the information only indirectly, through executive agencies, congressional support agencies, advocates, constituents, or others. For more information on the critical roles of staff, readers are referred to the chapter by Brown in this volume and to Redman (1973) and Zweig (1979).

Formal Hearings. Subcommittees and full committees frequently hold public hearings to gain or highlight information. Results of evaluations are often summarized in testimony at these hearings. Hearings can provide the most direct channel of communication between evaluators and members of Congress, since in some instances the evaluator is given the opportunity to testify.

At least four factors, however, hinder the transmission of evaluation results at hearings. First, hearings are often partly a pro forma exercise. They provide a way of formalizing and publicizing arguments, but the members are often aware in advance of the basic arguments to be presented. Written copies of testimony are often available before the hearing. The questions that members ask of witnesses —and, in some cases, even the answers provided by witnesses—are sometimes arranged in advance. Members come and go during the course of a hearing, and while an important witness at a particularly important hearing may face a majority of the committee's members, it is not uncommon to testify before a dais at which only one or a few members are seated. Those who are absent rely on written copies of testimony, the transcript of the hearing, and staff reports to find out what they missed.

Second, staffs sometimes structure hearings to emphasize certain points and to bolster a particular position, not to provide a balanced range of views. This structuring can be manifested in both the scheduling and the selection of witnesses.

Third, it is rare for a witness to have enough time at a hearing to explain an evaluation study thoroughly. Experienced witnesses aim for about fifteen minutes of testimony, which allows clear explication of no more than three or four main conclusions and a handful of caveats and elaborations. Moreover, witnesses often have less time than that. Frequently, they are asked to summarize their testimony in a few minutes and to submit more detailed comments for the record. With luck or with advance planning with committee staff, a witness is sometimes able to use subsequent question-and-answer periods to elaborate, but sometimes—for example, toward the end of a long hearing or when another committee hearing or an important debate on the floor is occurring at the same time—there are few questions.

Fourth, evaluation results are often presented at a hearing not by researchers but by officials of the executive agency that funded the research, advocates, or others. These third parties often present either an incomplete or a biased overview of the results. This may be intentional, or it may reflect lack of expertise and technical training.

The Media. Evaluation research is frequently reported by various media, including not only the public media but also many specialized, limited-circulation newsletters. Such newsletters are widely read in Washington. While the reports that they contain are not always fully accurate, they are brief and comprehensible to a general audience, so their impact can be great.

Executive Agencies. Executive agencies—in particular, the Departments of Health and Human Services, Labor, and Education—play a critical role in regulating both the production and the use of evaluation research. They finance a substantial proportion of it, and with this power of the purse comes power to decide which programs to evaluate and how to evaluate them. (In various ways, by mandating studies of certain programs, for example, and by earmarking funds for evaluation, the Congress periodically reserves some of this control for itself. The Congress's involvement, however, is very limited, and it typically exerts very little or no control over the details of evaluation policy.) Moreover, the executive agencies are often the only point of contact between the government and those who conduct the research.

In many cases, evaluation research must pass through several qualitatively distinct levels of bureaucracy before it is transmitted by an executive agency to the Congress. The technical staff with whom most evaluation researchers interact contribute to the preparation of testimony, memos, or other transmissions, but the major decisions about what is to be transmitted and what is to be emphasized are likely to be made elsewhere. High-level administrative officials, the managers of the programs involved, supervisors of the research office, and offices of policy and legislative liaison may all be involved.

Given the complexity of the process, an agency's transmission of evaluation is not simply the forwarding of a completed study. Rather, there are innumerable opportunities for repackaging, changes in emphasis, and so on. Moreover, many of the decisions of this sort are made by individuals whose interests and skills are not those of evaluators and whose criteria are often political rather than technical.

Congressional Support Agencies. Four support agencies provide evaluative information to Congress: the General Accounting Office (GAO), the Congressional Research Service (CRS), the Office of Technology Assessment (OTA), and the Congressional Budget Office (CBO) (see the Editors' Notes). Their work in evaluation is diverse. It includes straightforward reporting and summarizing of existing studies, critiques of existing studies, critical syntheses of multiple studies, secondary analysis of existing data, and original research.

The involvement of support agencies in evaluation can have a critical effect on the impact of an outside researcher's work on legislation. A support agency may offer the Congress its own assessment of a program that may conflict with the assessment of the outside researcher or that of the executive agency that sponsored the outside evaluator's work. In addition, the support agency may serve as a critical channel by which the outside researcher's work reaches the Congress, albeit in interpreted and summarized form.

The involvement of support agencies in the use of evaluation adds an additional political element to the controversy: the differential prestige and credibility of the various organizational players. This element is described vividly in Brown's chapter in this volume. Support agencies are often more credible sources of information than executive agencies because they usually have no stake in the program in question. This rule, however, has exceptions, and the relative credibility of the various support agencies and executive agencies that participate in the assessment of given programs varies from subcommittee to subcommittee and even, in some cases, from program to program.

As in the case of executive agencies, the transmission of outside evaluations by support agencies is in most cases not a simple forwarding or summarizing of results; rather, it involves considerable synthesis and interpretation. Those who perform these tasks are often technically trained, but they are rarely specialists in evaluation. The clear exception to this is the Institute for Program Evaluation (IPE), a relatively new branch of the General Accounting Office, which is largely staffed by evaluation researchers. To date, however, IPE has focused more on the production of independent research than on the synthesis of work by others.

Interest Groups. Members of Congress and their staffs are constantly approached by groups and individuals representing a wide range of interests. These interest groups include industry lobbyists, trade and professional associations, advocacy groups, and groups of constituents with local concerns.

Providing information, including the results of evaluations, is one important function of interest groups. The information that they provide, moreover, is not always restricted to information that bolsters their position in a current debate, although it rarely includes information clearly damaging to their position. The advocate who provides a wide variety of information, including some that is neutral, is useful to the member and staff and stands to gain additional access as a result.

The evaluative information provided by interest groups is extremely diverse. Formal summative evaluations are one kind of information that these groups provide, but it is not the only kind, and when summative evaluations are provided, they are often of low quality or are misrepresented. Neither the low quality nor the misrepresentation necessarily represents bad faith; often, it only reflects a lack of technical expertise on the part of the interest group and its representatives.

The Interplay Between Channels. These six channels—staff, hearings, the media, executive agencies, congressional support agencies, and interest groups—are not independent, and information on any major issue generally flows through several. A member who is seriously concerned about an issue may request analyses by one or several congressional support agencies as well as a report from the executive agency that operates the program involved. These reports go to relevant staff members as well as the Congressman. Usually, they are made public shortly thereafter. Next, the member and staff often hold formal hearings on the issue, at which the agencies' testimony—often, a synopsis of their reports—is joined by testimony from diverse interest groups. In preparing for hearings, congressional staff members and the staff of the agencies concerned are likely to have extensive interaction, during which the content of the reports is clarified and elaborated. In the meantime, press reports on the agencies' reports are likely to affect the testimony by other witnesses.

How Does the Congress Make Use of Evaluation Research?

Four factors largely determine the ways in which the Congress makes use of evaluation research once obtained: the role of the Congress in mediating between conflicting interest groups; the fast, often frenetic, pace of congressional work; the resilience of established federal programs; and the lack of technical training of most members of Congress and their staffs.

Mediating Between Interest Groups. As noted earlier, because one function of Congress is mediating between competing interests, summative evaluations are only one of many factors that Congress considers in determining the value of a given program. Different interest groups have different reasons for considering a program valuable. Even when they agree on the program's goals, they sometimes present radically different evidence concerning its impact.

Thus, the reception that a congressional committee gives to an evaluation does not depend completely on the persuasiveness of the evaluation or on the skill with which it is presented. The relative importance of different interest groups and the strength of their views often lead Congressmen to form strongly held positions even before a relevant evaluation is presented. In addition, members of a congressional committee who lack technical expertise are likely to judge competing evaluation claims in part on the established credibility of different witnesses or agencies. Members of Congress are not generally likely to have opinions about the relative credibility of two evaluation specialists, but they do have opinions about the relative credibility and impartiality of the organizations or groups that present evaluations.

The Pace of Congressional Work. Although the Congress as a body sometimes moves at a snail's pace, its constituent parts—members, staffs, and committees—often work at a frenetic pace that is hard to imagine from the outside. This pace reflects the large number of issues that are before the Congress simultaneously, the large number of interest groups whose views on each issue must be heard, the large number of members between whom compromises must be engineered, and, in many instances, the large number of bills introduced to deal with a single issue. Moreover, members and staffs must often consider individual issues and programs at an extreme level of detail, making decisions not only about program effectiveness but also about legal issues, program oversight, program administration, and funding levels.

As a result of the array of issues and details that demand attention at any one time, members and staff have little time to ponder the results of evaluations. In cases where conflicting results are available or where evaluation results are ambiguous, the pace of congressional work can pose a serious impediment to the use of evaluation.

Resilience of Federal Programs. Federal programs are not wont to disappear once they are well established. The success of the Reagan administration during its first year in both eliminating some programs and reducing the scope of others should not obscure this fact. The most important thing about the success of the Reagan administration was that it was extraordinary. Moreover, it was only partial, as many programs targeted for extinction survived, in some cases without major cutbacks. For example, the administration proposed to fold both the massive Title I compensatory education program and the education for the handicapped program into block grants at substantially reduced levels of funding. Both survived as distinct programs; Title I received smaller cuts in funding than proposed, while funding for education for the handicapped remained roughly constant.

Once a program is established, a constituency quickly develops around it. This constituency comprises a wide range of groups who benefit in different ways from the continued existence of the program. These groups include the direct beneficiaries of the program, the organizations or professions that are paid to run it, the executive agency that administers it, Senators and Congressmen whose districts benefit more than most from the program, the congressional committees that authorize it (and whose power therefore depends in part on it), and the social scientists whose work derives from it. Once the iron triangle of congressional committees, executive agencies, and program beneficiaries has become established, it is difficult to eliminate a program or even to scale it back.

Because of this inherent resilience of federal programs, congressional committees are often interested in deciding not whether to abandon a program but how best to change it. In addition to changing the program's level of funding and scope of operations, a committee may be interested in making changes in the program's operation, either to improve its overall performance or to meet other political needs.

The information provided by a summative evaluation is often not particularly useful to a committee that is considering marginal changes in a program. A generally positive summative evaluation can contribute to a decision to expand the program, and a negative evaluation can contribute to a decision to slow its growth or to cut it back. Beyond that, however, summative evaluations often provide little relevant information. For example, they seldom provide insight into the most cost-effective means of operating the program, and they generally lack reliable evidence about differential effectiveness, that is, the relative effectiveness of variants of the program.

The absence of reliable information on differential effectiveness is often a particularly serious hindrance to constructive congressional use of evaluations. The need for such information is clear, whether the summative evaluation is positive or negative, because in either case it could be used to improve the performance of the program. In the case of a negative or ambiguous summative evaluation, however, the pressure to obtain information on differential effectiveness can be much greater, since such information could be used to argue against cutting back or eliminating the program. Armed with information on differential effectiveness, supporters of a program can point to the more effective program variants as evidence that the program has greater potential than the mean effect indicates.

Unfortunately, it is generally not apparent to congressional staff when summative evaluations do not provide reliable assessments of differential effectiveness, and it is sometimes not apparent to evaluators or to agencies reporting evaluations, either. (For a brief description of some of the general problems involved in assessing differential effectiveness, see Koretz, Vopava, and Darlington (1978) and Ginsburg and Koretz (1979)). As a result, committees are on occasion presented with assessments of differential effectiveness that are unreliable or even meaningless.

Lack of Technical Training. Congressmen and their staffs vary greatly in their educational background, but few are scientists, and very few are social scientists. This creates two problems for those who wish to present evaluation to the Congress in a way that is useful.

The first, and most obvious, problem is that few in the Congress and in congressional staffs understand the technical language of evaluation. In many cases, this is not an insurmountable problem, since much of the technical language can easily be eliminated. Some technical concepts, however, are truly difficult to express in nontechnical terms. These concepts can pose a formidable problem in the presentation of results.

The second problem is that the fundamentals of scientific method and research design are not obvious to many on the Hill. The necessary points can often be explained in terms comprehensible to a lay audience, but the necessity of doing so can make it very difficult to present complex results in a short time. Moreover, some critical issues, such as selection bias and the viability of alternative hypotheses, can be surprisingly difficult to explain. A particularly difficult aspect of the problem is that few on the Hill are familiar with probabilistic inference. The meaning of such terms as *statistical significance* and, in a technical sense, *confidence* is not apparent to a lay audience, while the basic concepts underlying them are both essential to evaluation and very difficult to explain in a short time. This problem is illustrated in the case history below.

A Case History: Congressional Assessment of the PSRO Program

An interesting instance of congressional use of evaluation is the case of the Professional Standards Review Organization (PSRO) program. This program, a peer review system designed to curtail health care use and costs in the Medicare and Medicaid programs while assuring quality of care, was never a large program by federal standards (its largest budget was less than $200 million per year). Nonetheless, it has been the subject of a great deal of evaluation effort and has been a controversial issue in the Congress for years. Moreover, congressional debate about the program has focused to a considerable degree on evaluations of the program.

History of the Program. The PSRO program, established by the Social Security Amendments of 1972, was one of many congressional responses to concern about the growing costs of the Medicare and Medicaid programs and about the quality of care purchased through these programs. (Medicare provides reimbursement for medical care for most of the elderly population and many disabled individuals. Medicaid provides reimbursement for medical care for certain subsets of the low-income population, such as families receiving Aid to Families with Dependent Children (AFDC). Medicare is entirely managed and financed by the federal government. Medicaid is largely managed by the states, within a framework of federal restrictions, and states contribute over 40 percent of the costs.) It operates through a network of about 200 PSROs—local or statewide independent organizations of physicians.

In practice, the PSRO program has devoted most of its resources to controlling the use and quality of inpatient hospital care, with control of use (and therefore of costs) absorbing substantially more of the program's resources than control of quality. In order to control hospital use, PSROs review the cases of individual Medicare and Medicaid patients to determine whether admission is justified and for how long continued hospitalization is warranted. Unless successfully appealed, denial of a hospital stay by a PSRO precludes federal reimbursement. PSROs also have powers (rarely used) to exclude hospitals and physicians from participation in the Medicare and Medicaid programs.

The PSRO program was controversial from the outset, and debate about it has continued. Both the Carter and Reagan administrations have been active in the fray but on opposite sides. The Carter administration considered the program important and pushed for its expansion, while the Reagan administration views it as an unwelcome intrusion into the market and has requested that it be abolished (Reagan, 1981).

History of Evaluation Efforts. Given its small size, the PSRO program has generated a remarkable quantity of evaluation research. The Department of Health and Human Services (HHS) published extensive annual evaluation reports, based largely on the work of outside contractors, starting in 1977. (These evaluations were initially undertaken while the department was still called Health, Education, and Welfare (HEW). For simplicity, the acronym HHS is used throughout this discussion, even when the events in question occurred before the department was renamed.) HHS's efforts included a national, quasi-experimental test of the program's effects on hospital use and costs, in which areas where PSROs had not yet been established served as a comparison group. The Congressional Budget Office performed two secondary analyses based on HHS data. The General Accounting Office produced a number of assessments of the program, including both outcome assessments and a type of process evaluation that might best be called management review. In addition, smaller-scale evaluations were conducted by individual PSROs, interested academics, and others. The scale of these evaluation efforts is suggested by the cost of the HHS evaluation, which was the most extensive. In 1979, HHS's evaluation report cost more than $2 million, of which $1.5 million was paid to contractors (Schaeffer, 1980). In comparison, funding for the PSRO program in 1979 was about $150 million.

Use of Evaluations of the PSRO Program. Much of the impetus for continued evaluation of PSROs stemmed from two things: the serious controversy in the Congress about the program, and the clear interest of one key congressional actor in using outcome evaluations as a critical criterion of the program's worth.

To understand the way in which the Congress used evaluations of the program, it is necessary to understand the way in which congressional committees divide responsibilities. Three different types of committees (or subcommittees)—authorizing, oversight, and appropriations committees—have strong interests in a program such as PSRO. Authorizing committees create programs, decide how they will be run, and "authorize" the maximum amount that can be spent on their operation. The authorizing committees of the PSRO program include the tax-writing committees—Ways and Means in the House and Finance in the Senate—as well as the Energy and Commerce Committee in the House. Oversight subcommittees are established by authorizing committees to investigate the performance of programs and to explore problems that bear on their areas of jurisdiction. Both Ways and Means and Energy and Commerce maintain oversight subcommittees, and both were active at various times in the PSRO debate. Finally, appropriations committees are responsible for determining the precise amount to be spent on each program.

The PSRO program originated in the Senate Finance Committee, and for many years, some of the program's staunchest supporters were on that committee's staff. The most active oversight role was played by the Subcommittee on Oversight of the House Committee on Ways and Means, which, until the present Congress, cast a highly critical eye on the program and called frequent hearings on the subject. The Oversight Subcommittee's interest and its explicit requests for information were a primary factor in maintaining the intense evaluation of the program. By 1980, the Appropriations Subcommittee in the House had been strongly affected by the Oversight Subcommittee's work, and its hearings that year made ample use of evaluations of the program.

In June 1978, six years after the enactment of the PSRO program's enabling legislation and several months after HHS published the first of its annual national evaluations of the program (Office of Planning, Evaluation, and Legislation, 1977), the Subcommittee on Oversight of Ways and Means held a key hearing on the program's effectiveness. Only two organizations testified: the GAO and HHS. Chairman Sam Gibbons opened the hearing by arguing that PSROs had failed to generate savings in health care costs and that he doubted that they ever could. GAO then presented a highly critical audit of self-evaluations by six PSROs. The six had claimed to generate savings in hospital costs of over $19 million dollars; GAO countered that almost $17 million of the putative savings were false, artifacts of accounting and other errors.

HHS's rejoinder was in part a disavowal of its own national evaluation and in part a promise of better to come. The Office of Planning, Evaluation, and Legislation (OPEL) report had not found much evidence of an aggregate effect of PSROs on hospital use, but it maintained that some PSROs were more successful than others in identifying unnecessary medical services. Moreover, it found that the costs of PSRO activities were high. In its testimony, HHS argued that steps were being taken to reduce the cost of PSRO activities and that ineffective PSROs would be terminated. These improvements held out the promise that the savings generated by the program would eventually exceed the costs of its operation.

Three aspects of this hearing are worth noting. First, most of the HHS personnel who testified were high-level staff; all were political appointees, and only one had research responsibilities—as the manager of the office that conducted HHS's relevant research efforts. Technical staff were present only to back up those testifying, by answering questions if those testifying could not. The contractors who conducted the evaluations were not called to testify. Second, HHS defended its program, although the available evaluation research gave it little support. Third, as often happens, the congressional support agency (GAO) and the executive agency (HHS) were cast as adversaries.

The adversarial relationship between the support and executive agencies is in part a function of their institutional roles, but it is also due to the structure of the hearings, and it can be enhanced by interactions between committee members and those testifying. The following exchange, for example, between Chairman Gibbons and Robert Derzon, administrator of the Health Care Financing Administration (HCFA)—the part of HHS responsible for both operating and evaluating the PSRO program—opened the HHS testimony:

Mr. Derzon: "Thank you very much. This is our first appearance before your Committee. We welcome the opportunity to be here. We welcome the opportunity to have heard [the GAO] report."

Mr. Gibbons: "I will bet you welcomed it like I welcomed my appendicitis" (Committee on Ways and Means, 1978, p. 21).

Chairman Gibbons emphasized the question of appropriate measures of the program's impact. He argued that it was the intent of Congress to stress cost containment over quality assurance, and he chastised HHS for distorting congressional intent by overemphasizing quality assurance in its implementation of the program. For the next several years, most debate both on the Hill and in the press focused on the cost containment issue. HHS and other supporters of the program continued to place considerable emphasis on quality assurance, however, perhaps because evidence concerning the program's effects on costs was never highly positive.

After this hearing, the Subcommittee on Oversight asked the Congressional Budget Office to look into HHS's evaluations of the program and to offer its own assessment of the program's effects. CBO, agreeing with Gibbons that cost control was the program's primary objective and considering measurement of effects on quality of care impractical, limited its own work to the cost containment aspects of the program. It produced two secondary evaluations of the program that in many ways paralleled HHS evaluations that were conducted at the same time. CBO used the HHS data and largely accepted HHS's methods (multiple regression in a quasi-experimental design), but it made some changes in methods in outcome assessment and in converting outcome measures into monetary terms.

Seen from the outside, the CBO and HHS evaluations seem quite similar. Not only did they use the same data and similar methods, but they agreed on at least three key points: First, PSROs appeared to reduce hospital use by Medicare patients by an amount in the range of 1.5 to 2 percent. Second, if PSROs generated any net savings for the government (that is decreases in Medicare costs, minus the cost of running the program), those savings were extremely small, amounting to less than .01 percent of relevant Medicare expenditures. Third, a substantial portion of the gross savings that PSROs generated for the government (that is, simple reductions in Medicare expenditures) resulted from transfer of Medicare costs to private patients in the same hospitals. The most important difference between the two evaluations concerned the relative impact of individual PSROs. HHS ranked all PSROs in effectiveness, while CBO argued on methodological grounds that such ranking was largely meaningless (Ginsburg and Koretz, 1979).

Nonetheless, the initial congressional debate focused on differences between the CBO and HHS reports. Two questions were central: Should the program be evaluated solely in terms of savings to the government, or should costs transferred to private patients be considered also? Did the program produce a slight net savings or a slight net loss? The first question was a matter of judgment, not of evaluation per se. The second was largely moot, since neither study estimated savings large enough to mark the program as a truly successful cost containment program.

In hearings before the Subcommittee on Oversight in June 1979 (Committee on Ways and Means, 1979), CBO and HHS answered both these questions differently. HHS focused on savings to the government and claimed that savings exceeded the program's costs by about 10 percent. CBO maintained that costs transferred to private patients should be taken into account and estimated savings (net of these costs) to be about 70 percent of program costs. CBO noted that, in any event, the savings estimated by HHS were extremely small and that the program could not really be considered successful even if the HHS estimate was the best one. CBO also stressed the large margin of error inherent in both estimates.

By answering these two questions differently, CBO and HHS appeared to be on opposite sides—HHS was arguing that the program did indeed save money, while CBO was arguing that it did not. That this disagreement was more apparent than real was often lost sight of in the debate, particularly as that debate was reflected in the press during the following year.

Several factors contributed to this. One was the adversarial structure of congressional debate. Synthesizing a consensus assessment from the two reports was not the task of Congress. Its task was to let the program's supporters and opponents fight it out and to see how much each side would win or lose. HHS was seen as having a political, as well as an evaluation, agenda: the administration strongly supported the program, and HHS was the administration's spokesman. The HHS evaluation provided ammunition for the program's supporters. CBO's negative appraisal provided ammunition for the other side.

A second contributing factor was the inability of many people on the Hill to understand probabilistic inference. CBO's brief explanation of the evaluations' similarity was couched in probabilistic terms: large margins of error and overlapping ranges. The difficulty in communicating such concepts in a useful way is indicated by the following question asked of CBO in response to its testimony by Congressman J. J. Pickle (D–Texas), a member of the committee:

> **Mr. Pickle:** "If your findings . . . are as full of uncertainties as you say, then your report doesn't mean much, does it? How can we believe then that they are very significant? What you are saying is that you really don't know whether you are saving or not, is that what you are saying?" (Committee on Ways and Means, 1979).

Ironically, one of the truly important differences between the evaluations—the assessments of the relative effectiveness of individual PSROs—received little attention at this point in the controversy, although both CBO and HHS had stressed differential effectiveness in their testimony for its relevance to the potential ability of HHS to use evaluation results to improve the program's aggregate performance. That this disagreement received little attention certainly did not reflect a general disinterest in the question. On the contrary, both the administration and some members of Congress repeatedly raised the issue of improving the overall performance of the program by weeding out ineffective PSROs or by having ineffective PSROs emulate successful PSROs. Indeed, one prominent Finance Committee staff member vehemently criticized the CBO evaluation for focusing on the average or overall performance of the program, rather than demonstrating the range of effectiveness of various PSROs.

Two factors, however, mitigated against active debate about CBO's assertion that current assessment of the relative effectiveness of individual PSROs was largely meaningless. First, at that time, the Congress had no questions before it that specifically required information on differential effectiveness. Second, and probably far more important, CBO's argument was technically complex, poorly understood even among evaluators, and not intuitively compelling. The technical arguments involved (Ginsburg and Koretz, 1979) were less well understood than most of those involved in the argument over the program's overall effect. In the end, CBO's initial testimony on the subject amounted to just an assertion that differential effectiveness had not been assessed reliably.

During the next two years, both CBO and HHS presented their assessments of the PSRO program at several hearings before the Ways and Means and Finance committees. The arguments remained basically similar, although there were changes in emphasis. HHS used newer data to update its evaluation and issued the more optimistic estimate that savings generated by the program exceeded program costs by about 27 percent (Health Care Financing Administration, 1979). CBO likewise updated its assessment, but the result was slightly more pessimistic than its first assessment (Koretz, 1981).

In its updated evaluation, CBO attempted to distinguish more explicitly between what might be called *evaluation differences* (for example, differences in effect-size estimates) and the differences in interpretation that had been a central aspect of the controversy. As noted earlier, one point of controversy concerned the appropriate measure of savings (specifically, whether costs transferred from the government to private patients should be counted as savings). In addition, there was substantial controversy concerning the appropriate delineation of program costs. CBO, accordingly, used each combination of savings and costs in translating its outcome assessment into monetary terms (Koretz, 1981). This approach may have helped to lessen the artificial adversarial relationship between the two evaluations, but it also generated a level of complexity at the bottom line that many in the press and some on the Hill found confusing. This reporting strategy made misinterpretation of the CBO report less likely by those knowledgeable about the program, but it also made the evaluation more difficult for others to understand.

Although hearings and the occasional publication of formal reports gained attention from the press, much of the essential impact of the CBO and HHS evaluations occurred behind the scenes, in interactions with congressional staff. Although CBO's most critical staff contacts were with the Subcommittee on Oversight of Ways and Means, which had formally requested CBO's work, other staffs also played an important role. Staff members provided feedback to CBO that helped CBO tailor its work to the needs of the Congress. In turn, CBO provided staff members with a great deal of information through memos, drafts, and phone conversations. In at least one instance, CBO's evaluation figured prominently in a subcommittee's deliberations and hearings about the program, even though CBO did not provide any formal testimony to that subcommittee. Rather, information was transmitted informally at the staff level and was confirmed only at the end by a formal exchange of letters.

Following the election of President Reagan, the position of the PSRO program changed abruptly. The new administration considered PSROs an unsuccessful and unwarranted intrusion of government into the market for health care. Citing CBO's evaluation (inaccurately) to substantiate its claim that the program was a failure, the administration proposed to reduce the program's funding by almost 60 percent in 1982 and to terminate federal funding by 1984 (Office of Management and Budget, 1981; Reagan, 1981). The initial reduction in funding was to be accomplished by eliminating the least effective PSROs (Office of Management and Budget, 1981). Overnight, HHS, which had been the program's defender on the Hill, became the advocate of its elimination.

Since the administration's proposed initial reductions in the program were to be based on the relative performance of PSROs, assessment of differential effectiveness became a central issue. CBO returned to the issue in subsequent testimony before the Ways and Means and Finance Committees (Ginsburg, 1981). Some of the more straightforward problems in such assessment were described, while the more technical problems were ignored. In subsequent conversations with staff, the issue took a more pragmatic form: To what degree would HHS efforts to rank PSROs succeed in eliminating the least effective ones? CBO's position was that such efforts would meet with only limited success.

Impact of the Research on the Debate and the Program

Any assessment of the effects of this intense Congressional use of evaluation is necessarily subjective. Nonetheless, it seems clear that it had a substantial effect on the nature of the debate, and it seems likely that it also had some effect on the fate of the program.

Effects on the Debate. One of the clearest effects of congressional use of the PSRO evaluations stemmed not from what I called earlier an evaluation difference but from a difference in interpretation. That is, the difference between HHS and CBO interpretations of the savings generated by the program focused debate on economic issues central to assessing benefits that accrue from decreasing beneficiaries' use of services, not to assessing decreased use.

The key issue was the difference between fixed and variable costs. Fixed costs (such as mortgage debts) do not vary over the short term as the consumption of services varies. Variable costs (such as laundry costs) do vary with the consumption of services. Evaluation of savings generated by changes in use requires assessing the percentage of costs that are fixed, how long they remain fixed, and who bears them if use declines. Moreover, it is necessary to decide whether costs that are borne by others when fixed costs are transferred are relevant to assessment of savings. All these issues became central to the debate over the value of the PSRO program. Moreover, since the same issues arise in judging many other programs, it is possible that heightened awareness of them created by the PSRO debate will influence other congressional debates in the future.

The prominence of evaluations in the debate also led to explicit discussion of some issues of evaluation per se (such as selection bias) and led to greater awareness of such issues among staff and members. The most striking result was a short-lived effort, discussed below, to mandate both internally valid studies of the program's effects and a program implementation process that would permit such studies. Whether the greater awareness will persist, however, and whether it will have appreciable effects on future congressional use of evaluations is not clear.

Finally, it is possible that the salience of the summative evaluations buttressed the tendency of the Congress to pay more attention to the program's cost containment function than to its quality assurance function. Recall that there was relatively little evaluation of the latter, in large part because of technical difficulties. Accordingly, the debate over conflicting (or apparently conflicting) evaluation results focused on cost containment.

The potential of evaluation to shift the focus of debate to evaluable outcomes is a very troubling problem. In this instance, the issue is moot, since it seems clear that the initial intent of Congress was to make cost containment the primary goal of the program. In general, however, the issue need not be moot, as the importance of IQ in evaluations of Head Start makes clear. Researchers evaluating Head Start were often led to focus on IQ by purely practical concerns, such as the ready availability of such measures (Zigler, 1973) or the necessity of finding measures comparable across studies (Bronfenbrenner, 1974; Lazar and others, 1977), not necessarily by a belief that raising IQ was the sole or primary goal of the program. Nonetheless, the salience of evaluations of IQ change seem to have shaped debate about the program (Datta, 1976).

The role of evaluation in influencing the issues that are debated does not have to be negative. In a recent discussion of the usefulness of evaluation to federal policy making, Kennedy (1981, p. 9) cites a series of important education evaluations to argue that "Instead of resolving issues or answering predefined questions, these studies probably helped [to] *clarify* the issues and define the questions and the alternatives" (italics in the original). Moreover, she argues that this is desirable—an "enlightenment function" (p. 26). While there is clearly substance to Kennedy's argument, it is equally clear that evaluators, in the pursuit of the evaluable, can distort the debate.

Effects on the Program. The generally pessimistic nature of the major evaluations—recall that even the most optimistic failed to find a substantial effect on expenditures for health care—was not sufficient to doom the program. Even when the Reagan administration proposed phasing out the program, it survived: The Omnibus Budget Reconciliation Act of 1981 allows HHS to close no more than 30 percent of the existing PSROs in fiscal year 1982.

Nonetheless, it is probably safe to conclude that congressional use of evaluation helped to limit the program's growth while the Carter administration was seeking to expand it. It also seems likely that, although the HHS and CBO evaluations agreed on many basic points, the HHS evaluation, if presented alone, would have served the program's supporters. The CBO version of the evaluation gave credibility to the view that the program might not be saving even trivial amounts of money and highlighted the fact that even the HHS evaluation was not truly optimistic.

Why, then, did the program survive? Part of the answer may lie in the fact that both of the major evaluations held forward the possibility of improving the program's performance, and HHS was always able to present steps then under way to improve it. Given congressional concern about rapidly increasing Medicare and Medicaid expenditures, one could make strong arguments in favor of maintaining a cost containment program that held out promise for the future, even if current savings were small.

It is also likely, however, that the program survived in part for reasons that have nothing to do with the program itself but that characterize the role of evaluation in the congressional process. As noted earlier, Congress does not primarily act as a judge. Rather, as members fight to protect interests that are important to them, the institution moves as a whole to reconcile competing claims. In such a context, evaluations are used to strengthen arguments on both sides, and they are more likely to change the votes of members who are weakly committed or uncommitted than those of members whose position is strongly held.

CBO's repeated explanations of the inability of existing evaluations to assess differential effectiveness had little effect. Once the Reagan administration's proposal had made differential effectiveness directly relevant to congressional decision making, the time required to generate reliable information became prohibitive from the congressional perspective.

Increasing the Validity of Evaluations: The Satterfield Amendment

A little-noticed effect of evaluations of the PSRO program was a short-lived attempt by the Congress to require that future PSRO activities be implemented in a way that permitted more valid evaluations.

In its initial report and testimony on PSROs, CBO stressed that possible problems of selection bias cast doubt on all evaluations of the program, since the program was initially implemented through a form of self-selection. This argument struck at least one staff member as critical, and the result was an amendment offered by Representative David Satterfield (D–Virginia), who then sat on one of the program's authorizing subcommittees, to preclude such ambiguities in future assessments of the program. PSROs had yet to extend monitoring to several other kinds of health care that were their responsibility under law. The Satterfield amendment would have controlled that expansion to provide for more valid evaluation.

As eventually incorporated into the Omnibus Reconciliation Act of 1980, the Satterfield provision stipulated that PSROs could only extend monitoring to other kinds of health care if permitted to do so by the Secretary of HHS. The Secretary had only two grounds for granting permission: if the PSRO had been "chosen by a statistically valid method that will permit a valid evaluation of the cost-effectiveness of such review to review particular health care services" or if such review had already been demonstrated effective "based upon such an evaluation, or upon an evaluation of comparable statistical validity" (Section 924).

The reference to "statistically valid methods" of selecting PSROs was clarified in a committee print (a document that accompanies most bills to clarify congressional intent). The committee print noted the need to have experiental and control groups, to choose these groups in such a way as to maximize the similarities between them, and to choose the groups "in a way which permits a comparison that is, in the statistical sense, unbiased" (Committee on Interstate and Foreign Commerce, 1980). Language specifically referring to random assignment was proposed but not incorporated into the report.

Unfortunately, this provision did not last long enough to affect the program, let alone to serve as a precedent for other programs. It was repealed by a provision in the Omnibus Budget Reconciliation Act of 1981. The desire for improved evaluation—which has only a long-term payoff—lost out to the desire to have a more rapid expansion of PSRO activities.

What Can an Evaluator Do?

As the preceding case history illustrates, evaluation research will often be eagerly received, and it may even be actively sought out, by people on the Hill, and it can easily become a central part of congressional debate. Accordingly, evaluators who would like to make their research useful in the policy-making process may wish to keep the congressional audience in mind when designing and reporting their work.

The suggestions that follow touch on both these stages of research, but they focus primarily on the stage of presentation, since it is at that stage that many evaluators will find that they can do the most to improve the usefulness of their work to the Congress. Many of these suggestions will be useful not only in presenting work to the Congress but also in making research useful to policy makers in general.

Design. For the evaluator fortunate enough to be able to consider an eventual congressional audience while work is still in the design stage, the preceding discussion holds one clear suggestion: Give serious throught to ways of generating reliable, relevant assessments of differential effectiveness. Such information is often critical in congressional debate, but by the time that point is reached, there is often no feasible way of generating reliable information in the time available.

Throughout the design stage, not just in choosing ways of assessing differential effectiveness, the researcher may find it helpful to learn about both the original intent of the program and the subsequent debate about it. The original intent can be learned from the introductory sections of the relevant statutes and, in far more detail, from the accompanying committee prints. The nature of subsequent debates can be learned in a number of ways: by looking through records of hearings, by talking to appropriate people in congressional support agencies and executive agencies, and by talking directly to congressional staff.

Presentation. At the stage of presentation, researchers should keep two goals in mind: Maximizing the comprehensibility of their work to a lay audience, and minimizing the potential for distortion as their work is interpreted and summarized in the congressional process. Steps that are taken to meet one of these goals will usually help to meet the other.

Be Brief and Include the Most Important Points in a Summary. The briefer the report and the better its summary, the more likely it is to be read, and the greater the chance that its main points will be understood and remembered.

Two basic guidelines are helpful in reducing a report to its essentials. First, the writer should feel that he or she has to justify the inclusion of material, not the exclusion of material. When in doubt, discard. Second, if detail and tangents are important, they are often best relegated to appendices and footnotes, where they will be available to the technical reader. In the narrative, they are an impediment to the lay reader.

Distill the most important conclusions and caveats into a summary that is no more than a half dozen single-spaced pages. If they do not fit, select a smaller set. The summary should be the most carefully written part of the evaluation report, since it will probably be the only part that many read. The summary should always be placed at the front of the report to maximize the chances that a reader pressed for time will note the most important points.

Write Everything Backwards. Conclusions and principle caveats should almost always be presented first, with supporting detail following. This crucial strategy is basically the opposite of standard academic style, which causes the reader to recapitulate the writer's own analytical experience. First comes the statement of the problem as it was perceived at the start of the research, together with a description of the author's hypotheses. Next comes a description of the details of the analytical process. At the end of all this, the patient reader is rewarded with the writer's conclusions. A typical Congressional reader lacks both the patience and the technical expertise for such an odyssey.

In contrast, in reports prepared for policy makers, each unit of a report—whether the paper as a whole or a chapter, section, or single paragraph—should begin with conclusions or other essential points. Follow these points with detail that explains them and provides elaboration.

Separate Necessary from Unnecessary Technical Points. Surprisingly few technical points must be included in the text to enable a reader to follow the story. Most technical points are not essential and should be relegated either to a footnote or to an appendix.

The rationale for removing most technical points from the text is simple: Most readers on the Hill do not understand them. Technical points that pepper the text are both a distraction and an incentive to discontinue reading. Placing technical points in appendixes or footnotes serves an important documentary function and allows the rare technically adept reader to draw independent conclusions about the study's merits.

Explicitly Tie the Study to Policy Issues. Since policy issues can change rapidly, this is not always possible. When it is possible, however, the writer should explain the study's relationship to policy questions early in the report (Zweig, 1979). This gives policy makers a reason for reading the report and a framework for assimilating it.

Avoid Jargon and Use Nontechnical Expressions for Key Concepts, Especially Probabilistic Concepts. In many instances, jargon is easily replaced with straightforward, nontechnical expressions that are far less likely to be misunderstood. For example, the term *interaction* is likely to be misconstrued (often as a synonym for *joint effect*) but is easily avoided. Phrases like *"There was an intervention-by-sex interaction"* or *Intervention interacted with sex* can be replaced by *Intervention had substantially more effect among males than among females*. Similarly, the phrase *The study has little external validity* is meaningless to many on the Hill, whereas *The study's results cannot be generalized to the entire population* or *The study's results are probably not applicable to many other program sites* are easily understood. Certain key notions, however—particularly probabilistic concepts—can be extremely difficult to express in plain English. It is essential to do so, however, since terms like *statistical significance* will, more often than not, be ignored or misconstrued, and without them, the basic conclusions of a study often cannot be communicated accurately.

One way of dealing with this dilemma is to stress the degree of confidence that the audience should have in the results. Depending on the instance, this can be done in several ways: by establishing a range of estimates, by describing the level of significance (that is, explaining the probability of obtaining any given positive result by simple chance if the program was actually ineffective), by describing alternative explanations and why they are or are not plausible, or by presenting sensitivity analyses.

A particularly thorny problem is posed by questionable null results. It is often difficult for lay audiences to understand why null results often should not be considered conclusive. Explaining the scientific logic of disconfirming a null hypothesis is not likely to help, but explaining study-specific factors that call a null result into question—for example, error-prone measurement—can be useful.

It may be helpful to keep in mind that the Congress is likely to find evaluation useful when it lessens ambiguity and provides a clear rationale for a position or a vote. Evaluation results, however, being probabilistic, are ambiguous by their very nature. Moreover, our training as evaluation researchers teaches us, as it should, to search this ambiguity out and to express it fully. It is difficult to be clear enough about the results to remove ambiguity (when the research justifies that), while nonetheless describing the uncertainties in a way that is both honest and comprehensible.

State the Limitations of the Research. Quite apart from the uncertainties inherent in probabilistic research, most evaluation research has definite limitations. These should be stated clearly, so that the audience understands what questions the research addresses and what questions it doesn't address. The lack of a clear statement of a study's limits is a common complaint of congressional staffers (Zweig, 1979).

Three types of limitations are particularly important. First, most evaluations consider only a subset of a program's goals, and this can be explained at the outset. Second, it is important to explain how generalizable the results are. Do they apply only to a subset of program beneficiaries or to a subset of program sites or variants? When evaluations are based on demonstration projects, the answer to these questions is generally positive. Third, do the results answer—reliably—any policy-relevant questions of differential effectiveness, such as the relative effectiveness of different program sites or variants, or the differential effects on different categories of beneficiaries? This last question is not always relevant, depending on the context, but when it is germane, it can be invaluable to have the answers explicit at the outset.

Give the Report to a Lay Reader. This is a good acid test. If an intelligent, well-educated reader, perhaps familiar with the program but with no technical training, cannot understand the essential points of the report, it needs revision.

Conclusion. All these suggestions have a common thread: By keeping the nature of the congressional audience in mind and by concentrating on communicating with this audience—even at the expense of expressing some of the less important nuances of a study—one can increase the odds that an evaluation will be noticed, understood correctly, and used in the legislative process and in other policy-making contexts as well.

References

Bronfenbrenner, U. *A Report on Longitudinal Evaluations of Preschool Programs.* Vol. II. *Is Early Intervention Effective?* (OHD-74-25) Washington, D.C.: Department of Health, Education, and Welfare, 1974.

Committee on Interstate and Foreign Commerce. *Medicare and Medicaid Amendments of 1980: Report of the Committee on Interstate and Foreign Commerce, U.S. House of Representatives. To Accompany H.R. 4000.* Washington, D.C.: U.S. Government Printing Office, 1980.

Committee on Ways and Means. *Professional Standards Review Organizations. Hearing before the Subcommittee on Oversight of the Committee on Ways and Means, House of Representatives.* (Serial 95-93). Washington, D.C.: U.S. Government Printing Office, 1978.

Committee on Ways and Means. *Review of PSRO Medical Cost Control. Hearing Before the Subcommittee on Oversight of the Committee on Ways and Means, House of Representatives.* (Serial 96-36). Washington, D.C.: U.S. Government Printing Office, 1979.

Datta, L. "The Impact of the Westinghouse/Ohio Evaluation on the Development of Project Head Start." In C. Abt (Ed.), *The Evaluation of Social Programs.* Beverly Hills, Calif.: Sage, 1976.

Ginsburg, P. B. Statement before the Subcommittee on Health, Committee on Finance, U.S. Senate, March 23, 1981.

Ginsburg, P. B., and Koretz, D. M. *The Effects of PSROs on Health Care Costs: Current Findings and Future Evaluations.* Washington, D.C.: Congressional Budget Office, 1979.

Health Care Financing Administration. *Professional Standards Review Organization 1979 Program Evaluation.* Washington, D.C.: Health Care Financing Administration, Department of Health and Human Services, 1979.

Kennedy, M. M. "Assumptions and Estimates of Evaluation Utility." *Educational Researcher,* 1981, *10* (10), 6-9, 26.

Koretz, D. M. *The Impact of PSROs on Health Care Costs: Update of CBO's 1979 Evaluation.* Washington, D.C.: Congressional Budget Office, 1981.

Koretz, D. M., Vopava, J., and Darlington, R. B. "Matching Early Intervention Programs to Children: Some Methodological Limitations." In B. Brown, Chair, *Matching Early Intervention Programs to Children.* Symposium presented at the annual meeting of the American Association for the Advancement of Science, Washington, D.C., February 1978.

Lazar, I., Hubbel, V. R., Murray, H., Rosche, M., and Royce, J. *The Persistence of Preschool Effects.* Washington, D.C.: Administration for Children, Youth, and Families; Department of Health, Education, and Welfare, September 1977.

Office of Management and Budget. *Fiscal Year 1981 Budget Revisions: Additional Details of Budget Savings.* Washington, D.C.: U.S. Government Printing Office, 1981.

Omnibus Budget Reconciliation Act of 1980 (P. L. 96-499), House Report 96-1479, 96 Cong. 2 sess. (1980).

Office of Planning, Evaluation, and Legislation. *PSRO: An Evaluation of the Professional Standards Review Organization* (77-12). Washington, D.C.: Health Services Administration Department of Health, Education, and Welfare, 1977.

Reagan, R. *America's New Beginning: A Program for Economic Recovery.* Washington, D.C.: The White House, Office of the President, February 18, 1981.

Redman, E. *The Dance of Legislation.* New York: Simon & Schuster, 1973.

50

Schaeffer, L. Statement before the Subcommittee on Labor–HEW, Committee on Appropriations. In Committee on Appropriations, *op. cit.*

Zigler, E. F. "Project Head Start: Success or Failure?" *Children Today,* 1973, 2 (7), 1–36.

Zweig, F. "The Evaluation World View of Congressional Staff." In F. Zweig (Ed.), *Evaluation in Legislation.* Beverly Hills, Calif.: Sage, 1979.

Daniel Koretz is a policy analyst with the Congressional Budget Office, United States Congress, where he has worked in the areas of health and education.

In its role as a broker between the scientific community and Congress, the Office of Technology Assessment evaluates the soundness of scientific conclusions for policy makers and ensures that research findings are included in formative policy analysis.

The Role of the Evaluation Research Broker

Pamela Doty

This chapter examines two policy-oriented evaluation studies carried out for Congress by the Office of Technology Assessment (OTA). As case studies, they illustrate some of the opportunities and problems involved in using scientific and social research findings in the policy-making process. More important, however, a description of how these two studies were carried out highlights the value of the brokering role that in-house research and analysis units play in synthesizing scientific data and findings in forms that are accessible, understandable, and useful for policy makers.

OTA Research Broker

Requests for OTA studies typically are made by the chairmen of standing committees of the House and Senate. (Unlike the General Accounting Office (GAO) or the Congressional Research Service (CRS), OTA does not carry out studies at the request of individual

The author is grateful to Daniel Koretz, Claudia Sanders, and Larry Miike for their useful comments on earlier drafts of this chapter. Larry Miike was the project director of both OTA studies described here.

L. Saxe, D. Koretz (Eds.). *New Directions for Program Evaluation: Making Evaluation Research Useful to Congress,* no. 14. San Francisco: Jossey-Bass, June 1982.

Congressmen or Senators.) Requests for studies must be approved by the Technology Assessment Board (TAB), which considers the priority of the proposed study in the light of OTA's annual operating budget of approximately $10 million. To remove OTA as far as possible from partisan politics, the TAB has twelve seats, which are split evenly among Senate and House, Republicans and Democrats.

As its name suggests, OTA's legislatively mandated mission is to assess or evaluate the likely consequences—both beneficial and harmful—of technological change. In this context, OTA is authorized to explore not only the physical and biological but also the economic, social, and political effects of applying scientific knowledge.

Technology assessment is what a sociologist would characterize as OTA's manifest function. An organization's manifest function (Merton, 1968) is its officially recognized and sanctioned purpose or goal, as stated in its charter or, in OTA's case, in its legislative history. A latent function is any other activity that the organization can be observed to engage in as it goes about its day-to-day business.

Sociologists love to uncover latent functions, and I, as a sociologist, am no exception, which explains why I have chosen to write about OTA's role as a research broker, not about technology assessment. This is not to say that research brokering and technology assessment are unrelated. Indeed, virtually every OTA technology assessment involves research brokering, simply because it is done for the Congress. Not every instance of research brokering, however, involves technology assessment.

Obviously, in a certain sense, every study that OTA does is a technology assessment. Moreover, OTA staff would not quibble about the definition of technology assessment if that meant turning down a study requested by a congressional committee. According to the official definition, however, a technology assessment is not just any kind of policy-relevant study that has something to do with science or technology.

The official definition of technology assessment, which appears on the back cover of every OTA report, is that its function is to "help legislative policy makers anticipate and plan for the consequences of technological change and to examine the many ways, expected or unexpected, in which technology affects people's lives. The assessment of technology calls for exploration of the physical, biological, economic, social, and political impacts which can result from applications of scientific knowledge."

Research Brokering Defined

In contrast, *research brokering,* as the term will be used, occurs when persons with scientific training evaluate or interpret scientific research findings, theories, or models for policy makers in such a way that the scientific input becomes relevant to policy making. There is a considerable professional literature on technology assessment, and those interested are referred in particular to Banta and Behney (1981) and Coates (1977, 1979). On the other hand, the literature on research utilization that refers specifically to the brokering function performed by OTA and similar organizations is scant (Hanft, 1981; Havelock, 1968; Meltzer, 1980; Rich, 1979).

Neither of the two studies that I will describe in this chapter sought to anticipate the future consequences of new technological developments. Rather, they explained, evaluated, critiqued, and synthesized existing scientific knowledge in a policy-making context that was closely tied to specific legislative concerns.

Demystifying Science for a Lay Audience

At the simplest level, our research brokering involved the explication and demystification of scientific terms, models, and theories on behalf of a scientifically untrained audience. At times this meant, quite literally, translating jargon into English. When the use of jargon is unavoidable, OTA reports usually include a glossary defining these problematic terms. The broker's role in demystifying science also involves explaining how a particular scientific finding was arrived at and evaluating whether the methodology was sound and the data were reliable. Thus, the analysis considers the assumptions that make up a model or theory and determines whether they are credible.

Research brokering as demystification comes to the fore when a congressional committee requests an OTA analysis, primarily so that members and staff can judge how much weight or credence to give to an argument or a piece of evidence. Demystification can be particularly useful to policy makers in the case of the numerical estimates (of everything from how many untapped barrels of oil remain in the earth to how many Americans could survive a nuclear attack) that are basic ammunition in the policy wars.

The OTA report on forecasts of physician supply and requirements, on which I worked, entailed an explication and critique of the executive branch's official estimate of the number of physicians that the United States would require in 1990. The study was jointly requested by the Senate and House committees in connection with debate over reauthorization of the Health Manpower Act. The most hotly debated issue was whether capitation grants to medical schools should be continued. Capitation grants are based on the number of students enrolled. They were originally intended, in the context of a perceived nationwide physician shortage, to provide financial incentives to medical schools to increase enrollments. As is often the case, political support for the subsidies persisted, despite mounting evidence not only that the physician shortage had been overcome but that the United States could well face a physician surplus in years to come. Though the capitation grants represented only a small fraction of medical revenues and thus were not necessary for most schools to exist, they were popular with medical school deans, because they were a source of discretionary funds.

The Political Context

Interestingly, within the Congress, most of the support for continuation of capitation payments came from a contingent of liberal Democrats whom one might not expect to be supporters of the medical establishment. Their principal argument in favor of capitation grants was that blacks, women, and other minorities would be less likely to be admitted to medical school in their absence. However, capitation grants were not awarded on the basis of minority enrollments. If the objective is to increase enrollments among these groups, special scholarships seem more to the point. The concern seemed to be that medical schools would reduce the size of their student enrollments if capitation payments were cut. In turn, this would reduce the size of the enrollment of women and minorities. However, there was no clear evidence that medical schools would react to the withdrawal of capitation grants by cutting back on enrollments. Informal soundings of medical school deans conducted by members of OTA's advisory panel indicated that, if they occurred, retrenchments would be made for reasons independent of the fate of capitation grants.

Another argument made in favor of continuing capitation grants was that their maintenance constituted potential leverage that the federal government could use to achieve some as yet undetermined objectives. As noted earlier, the main attraction of capitation grants for the medical schools was that no strings were attached. If schools were required to pursue admissions policies that they disliked or subjected to burdensome reporting regulations, it seems likely that many would decide that the amount of money involved was not worth it.

The Report's Impact

The final outcome of the debate was a decision to phase out capitation grants gradually. What part the OTA report on physician supply and requirements had in this decision is difficult to ascertain, but that the report had very little direct influence on this decision seems likely. As the preceding discussion indicates, the lineup in Congress over capitation payments took place primarily along ideological and political lines. It seems likely, moreover, that the conflict was part of a broader, ongoing struggle for power between leaders and factions of liberal Democrats over how the key issues in health policy should be defined and by whom. The Kennedy contingent held to the old liberal agenda. They wanted the focus to remain on issues such as minority representation in the medical profession, increased training of family practitioners (for which capitation grants might possibly attract the medical schools), and more federal support for physicians in underserved geographic areas. The Waxman camp (Representative Henry Waxman, D-California, is Chairman of the Health and Environment Subcommittee of the House Energy and Commerce Committee) represented a different breed of liberal Democrat, not lacking in social conscience but concerned about potential negative effects of the rapidly expanding physician supply, such as overuse of health services and rising costs.

All this is not to say, however, that the OTA report had no policy impact; rather, its impact was elsewhere. The nature of that impact aptly illustrates Carol Weiss's (1977) point that the major impact of policy research often is its influence on how policy makers perceive or define issues and problems.

First, the OTA report discredited the federal government's official estimate (by HEW's Bureau of Health Manpower) of the number of physicians that the nation would require by 1990—in particular, the assertion that physician supply and requirements would be "substantially in balance" in 1990. Interestingly, although the widespread public perception was one of shortage, most members of Congress and staffers knowledgeable about health manpower issues were aware that medical schools had for some time been training far more physicians than the population growth justified. They were aware of studies which pointed out that past policy initiatives to expand medical education would result in a physician surplus starting around 1990, if not sooner. The OTA study was, however, the first such study to receive significant media attention, including major news articles by the *New York Times,* the *Washington Post,* and a column by Dan Greenberg. The OTA report was considered newsworthy for several reasons: OTA was a Congressional support agency, the official government estimates that OTA challenged were fresh in everyone's mind, and the OTA report indicated that the physician surplus in 1990 could well be larger than anyone had already anticipated.

The Graduate Medical Education National Advisory Committee (GMENAC) report was published five months later, in September

1980. It reached similar conclusions, although its estimate of the surplus was lower than OTA's, and it served to focus still more media attention on the issue of a potential physician surplus. Media attention alters the context of public awareness in which political debate takes place. Previous debate over medical manpower issues had taken place in the context of a nearly universal public belief that there was a national shortage of physicians. Politically, this meant that subsidies for medical education, particularly as continuation of an extensive policy, did not need to be justified or explained to the public. Indeed, a politician who favored withdrawing the subsidies could be seen to be acting in the interests of organized medicine, because one widespread popular explanation was that the physician shortage resulted from conspiracy by the AMA to limit the number of physicians and thereby ensure continued high fees. No doubt, there is a significant contingent of the public who still see medical education manpower issues in this light. However, media attention to the OTA and GMENAC reports means that the educated, politically active public will become increasingly aware that the physician shortage has been overcome and a surplus may be in the making.

In September 1980, *Esquire* magazine published an article (Welles, 1980) on narrowing career options available to the baby boom generation. This article in a mass circulation magazine cited the OTA report on forecasts of physician supply and requirements twice. The author seemed to feel that his point would surprise enough readers that he had to have an authoritative source. His point was that, in the coming decade, not even physicians could be certain that demand for their skills would ensure the present high medical incomes, because of their growing numbers.

Taking a Number Apart

The congressional request did not ask OTA to come up with its own estimate of 1990 physician requirements but to evaluate the forecasts and forecasting techniques of the authoritative sources for such estimates. In practice, this meant the official government estimates of physician supply and requirements issued periodically by the Bureau of Health Manpower in the Department of Health, Education, and Welfare (HEW), now Health and Human Services, and the estimates prepared by the Graduate Medical Education National Advisory Commission operating under the auspices of HEW. Although we did evaluate GMENAC's forecasting techniques favorably, it had not yet issued a report. Accordingly, we focused our evaluation on the estimates of aggregate physician supply and requirements issued by the Bureau of Health Manpower (BHM).

Explicating Assumptions. Our first task was to uncover the assumptions on which BHM estimates were based and explore how different assumptions would have affected the projected 1990 balance of physician supply and demand. We found that the BHM estimate of economic demand for physician services in 1990 was produced by projecting per capita use rates from 1975 onto the 1990 population. These figures were then adjusted for what the Bureau termed a long-term trend toward rising use of services, after analysis of historical changes in per capita utilization in data from the National Center for Health Statistics for the period 1968-1976. Thus, OTA separated projections of future use into projections based on population growth and changes in age, sex, and income distribution and projections based on long-term growth in use of physician services.

The BHM model was based on the assumption that supply and demand were in balance in 1975. For BHM, this simply provided a constant against which the relative magnitude of future changes could be measured. Our review of the literature found that previous estimates of appropriate utilization of physician services, which were based on a variety of different models (professional judgment, need-based, and economic demand-productivity models and HMO physician-patient ratios), reached the same conclusion: In 1975, the available physician supply of 378,000 was indeed sufficient in the aggregate to meet the nation's requirements for physician services. If the 1975 per capita use rates are applied to the 1990 population, demographic changes alone (that is, population increases plus changes in age, sex, and income distributions) lead to a 10 percent increase in demand for physician services. At current rates of physician productivity, this means that 37,000 additional physicians are required in 1990.

The BHM model also projected demand for 185,000 additional physicians in 1990 as a result of a long-term trend toward increased per capita use of physician services. We examined the statistical basis for this long-term trend, and our findings cast serious doubt on BHM methods. We discovered that BHM economists had chosen a procedure (regression analysis of 1968-1976 data on per capita physician visits) that amortized a one-time major increase in use of physician services during the late 1960s—which can be traced to the introduction of Medicare and Medicaid and concomitant expansion in employer-subsidized health insurance—over the entire eight-year period and then projected the resulting trend line fifteen years forward. What made existence of this trend especially dubious was that, if BHM had chosen to start its trend line in 1971, regression analysis would have produced a slight downward trend yielding a small decrease in the number of physicians required in 1990, when other anticipated demographic changes were also taken into account. In other words, OTA found that more than 80 percent of BHM's estimate of additional physicians required to meet demand for physician services in 1990 was the effect of a methodological error.

Policy Implications of the Physician Surplus. As a follow-up to this study, OTA was asked by the House Subcommittee on Health and the Environment to estimate the effect that a supply of 600,000 physicians in 1990 would have on national health expenditures. The results of this work were presented as testimony delivered during committee hearings in March 1980. The way by which we arrived at these estimates illustrates another facet of research brokering; namely, linking theoretical work in an academic discipline with policy analysis as practical problem solving.

The question of how growth in the physician supply by 1990 will affect national health expenditures is compounded by a major theoretical controversy in health economics. One school of thought holds that the traditional supply-demand equation applies as much to health care as to any other market commodity. Accordingly, as physician supply increases, the price per unit of service will drop, due to competition. The other argues that health care is not like other market commodities, in that demand is not a function primarily of what individual consumers decide that they want to buy and can afford. (See Greenberg, 1978, for material representing both sides of the debate.) Once an individual makes the initial decision to consult a physician, it becomes the physician, by virtue of his or her medical expertise, who decides how many services and what kinds the individual should receive. This school also argues that health insurance greatly reduces constraints imposed by patients'—and doctors'—perceptions of the care that the patient can afford.

According to this latter school of thought, individual physicians strive for a particular target income, which can be achieved by manipulating the variables at their disposal. In order to achieve their desired income, they can see more patients, raise their prices, or increase demand for their services from their patients by prescribing follow-up visits or diagnostic tests, by opting for surgery in cases where it is of uncertain benefit, and so on.

Obviously, the financial consequences of a supply of 600,000 physicians in 1990 would be quite different, depending on the theory that one adopts. Neither theory, however, provides much practical guidance on how to estimate national health expenditures in 1990. Most economists consulted indicated that lengthy and elaborate model building would be required. We had six weeks in which to complete the work. Moreover, the economists whom we consulted told us that there were no data relevant to the model. Accordingly, they advised us to tell the Congressional committee that had made the request that the question could not be answered in a scientifically responsible manner.

We were faced with a dilemma. OTA did not want to tell the Committee that we could not answer the question. But we also did not want to employ a methodology that we considered intellectually dishonest. Our solution to this dilemma illustrates the role that scientific expertise, mixed with creative common sense, plays in policy analysis.

We made the commonsense assumption that, at the very least, individual physicians in 1990 would want to earn as much money in constant dollars as physicians earned in the mid to late 1970s. We then found a reliable source of data on current physician incomes and on the relationship of physician's personal income to total billings. Multiplication yielded a total figure for the billings that 600,000 physicians would need to generate in 1990 in order to have incomes on a par with today's.

Next, we asked how realistic it was to assume that physicians in 1990 would be able to attain incomes equivalent in constant dollars at least to the 1978 median income of physicians. According to the "competition" school, since growth in supply of physicians would have greatly outpaced general population growth by 1990, physicians could not increase their income by serving more patients. Indeed, on the average, each physician would serve fewer patients. In turn, competition among physicians for patients would hold prices down—unless there was a great increase in individual Americans' demand for medical care. As already noted, however, household surveys by the National Center for Health Statistics indicate that the number of yearly physician visits per capita remained relatively constant across the population as a whole and even declined slightly in certain population subgroups during the 1970s. Barring enactment of a generous national health insurance plan, there is no reason now to anticipate a great upsurge in the average American's annual number of physician visits.

If, however, one adopts the induced demand hypothesis, one expects physicians to respond to the competitive pressures of expanding supply by increasing demand artificially and prescribing more services per patient. The issue then becomes how much demand physicians would want or be able to induce. If induced demand could compensate for the increased physician supply, the consequences of past policy to increase physician supply would be enormously expensive for the nation.

To answer this question, several research studies were examined. Analyzing Medicare data, Urban Institute researchers found that physicians responded to the Nixon administration's wage-price freeze by prescribing additional visits or procedures but that this induced demand was far from sufficient to make up for the losses in real income due to inflation that physicians experienced during the periods of wage-price freeze (Hadley and others, 1979). The researchers concluded that both the willingness and the ability of physicians to increase their income by increasing demand for their services from a fixed number of patients is real but far from limitless—much less than proponents of target income–induced demand theory lead us to expect.

Another study reviewed was Princeton University health economist Uwe Reinhardt's (1975) analysis of data on physician income and other practice characteristics in geographic areas of high and low physician density. In areas of high physician density, Reinhardt found, physicians deal with competition not by lowering fees but by lowering productivity and raising fees. In high-density areas, physicians charged higher fees per visit but saw considerably fewer patients than physicians in low-density areas. They were able to do this because the high-density areas were generally the more affluent urban and suburban areas, while the low-density areas were rural and considerably less affluent. Reinhardt's findings suggest that the belief that, as the physician supply grows, physicians will compete to attract patients by lowering their prices is naive.

Interpreting Results. We drew the conclusion that, as predictors of the consequences of greatly increased physician supply, both the competition model and the induced demand model are probably right and wrong in key aspects. The competition model is probably correct in predicting that physicians will not be as well off in 1990 as their 1978 counterparts. Patients, however, are unlikely to encounter lower physician fees as the result of increased competition. Fees could well be higher, in constant dollars, than they were in 1978. We concluded that adaptation to the competition for patients created by increased physician supply and constant demand is most likely to take the form of decreased physician case loads. Physicians, who traditionally have been "workaholics," will either cut back to more normal 40-hour workweeks, or they will spend more time with patients than the current average of ten minutes per patient. Probably they will engage in some combination of both these behaviors. One result could be that physicians would find salaried group practice more appealing. They might also be more willing to spend time counseling patients and involving them in decision making. Those who favor the growth of HMOs and group practice and who believe that physicians should spend more time with patients view the projected physician surplus as a positive social phenomenon, insofar as it favors these aims. In a less optimistic vein, given the small but nonetheless real tendency toward induced demand that Hadley's study uncovered, doctors in 1990 could be expected to fill at least some of the increased time that they spend with patients performing tests and procedures that are of dubious medical necessity and benefit.

Everyone agrees that if the expanding physician supply promotes higher fees and unnecessary and inappropriate use of physician services, it is negative. There is less consensus about the desirability of changes in physician productivity and the organization of medical practice that may result. If physicians see fewer patients but spend more time with each one, will the result be higher-quality care? Can such increments in quality ever be measured? If they can be measured, how much is a given unit of higher-quality care worth to society in higher medical costs?

The last question illustrates the inevitably normative aspects of the questions that we were considering. Sociology students are often taught that fact and value questions can and should be separated. However, as a research broker attempting to make scientific techniques and findings accessible and useful to political decision makers, I found that the factual and normative elements of policy issues were disturbingly intertwined. Consider that, because quality of medical care is not readily measurable, it tends routinely to be left out of scientific forecasts of the effects of particular policies. This means that, as decision making is increasingly based on or influenced strongly by scientific findings, important social values that cannot be dealt with scientifically will be routinely excluded from the decision-making process. Consider also that a forecast's conclusions are determined not only by the data but also by the assumptions on which the model is based. As the assumptions vary, so, in most cases, will the conclusions, sometimes by a very wide margin. Assumptions can be subjected to tests of logic and reasonableness based on past experiences, but when the assumptions concern future events (for example, effects of the passage of national health insurance on use of physician services), they cannot be confirmed by a definitive empirical test. When considering the future, one can take the position that anything is possible. To make a forecast that generates definite conclusions, or at least a finite range of conclusions, requires making certain assumptions about the future and rejecting others. On what basis do we make these assumptions? What determines the range of assumptions that are considered? Can these decisions be made on purely scientific grounds? If they cannot, then normative (or at least nonrational) choices fundamentally shape every scientific forecasting effort, although this occurs mostly unconsciously. To me, this suggests that, instead of insisting that scientific forecasts can and should be objective, we should simply step back on occasion to reconsider our basic assumptions. We should ask ourselves—not all the time, but occasionally—what variables we routinely exclude from our equations and why, as well as what assumptions we are unwilling to entertain and why.

One final note on the relationship of values to forecasting: those of us who worked on the forecast of physician supply and requirements could not help but observe that, to a certain extent, value judgments were built into the very language that we used. Terms like *surplus* and *requirements* carry normative connotations. After all, a certain number of physicians can only be referred to as a surplus if one has decided that there are too many physicians. Because of this, at several points during the study, we seriously considered replacing terms like *surplus* with value neutral terms. In the end, we had to reject that approach, because it would have made our findings unintelligible.

Research Brokering in Formative Policy Analysis

OTA's role as a research broker also involves carrying out formative policy analyses that take scientific input—in particular, academic research findings—into account. Formative policy analysis is the analysis that goes into shaping new social policies and programs. With relatively few exceptions, most of what usually goes by the name of evaluation research is retrospective evaluation of the effectiveness of policies and programs that have already been enacted and implemented. Although demonstration projects to test policy concepts before they are launched as major programs are becoming more common, it would be too expensive and too cumbersome to subject all new policies to this kind of evaluation. Thus, formative policy analysis is all the evaluation that many legislative proposals for major policy and program initiatives receive before they are enacted into law.

All four congressional support agencies do formative policy analysis. Only CRS and OTA, however, can be said to make extensive use of academic research findings in their formative policy analysis. One way academic research findings are brought into OTA's analysis is via the literature search capabilities of the Library of Congress. OTA, like CRS, also makes extensive use of informal telephone canvassing of the research community. Most researchers seem flattered to be called, and most OTA staff consider being able to call upon some of the most eminent research scientists one of the best aspects of their work.

OTA has two other important mechanisms for linking the academic research community to the policy process. One is the advisory panel. Each study has an advisory panel, composed mainly of eminent academics, but also, where appropriate, of representatives of industry, labor, consumers, and other interest groups. Unlike the National Academy of Sciences, OTA does not require panel members to reach consensus on or endorse study findings. Rather, the advisory panels serve primarily as sounding boards to ensure that all significant issues are addressed. In addition, advisory panels review draft and final reports and thereby perform a valuable quality control function. Finally, to the degree that the panel members are eminent researchers in their fields, they serve to keep OTA staff abreast of the latest research developments in the field, and they can orient OTA staff toward useful sources of data, as well as to recent or unpublished research.

Finally, of all congressional support agencies, OTA has the greatest pool of funds available for contracts with outside researchers. Although the contracts typically involve small amounts (under $10,000) and short periods of time (three to six months), they can be awarded on a sole-source basis, on short notice, without the competitive bidding and other requirements that make contracting by federal agencies a lengthy process. Some OTA programs rely extensively on outside contractors; others, much less so. A large study with multiple outside contractors, each of whom is responsible for a small piece of the whole, can pose serious managerial and quality control problems for project directors and program managers. Because of this, the appropriate balance between intra- and extramural research is a perennial matter for discussion and debate at OTA. The contracts do, however, create a significant interpenetration between OTA and outside academic and nonacademic research communities.

Focused Synthesis

The major methodology involved in formative policy analysis can be called focused synthesis. Superficially, focused synthesis looks like an academic literature review. An academic literature review is a summary of the state of the art of a given scientific specialty, with an emphasis on the most recent theoretical developments and empirical research. A focused synthesis, however, is more selective, in that it presents only the scientific findings that are relevant to particular policy questions. At the same time, focused synthesis is more eclectic than academic literature review, in that it entails putting scientific findings and theoretical perspectives together with other types of information—what Lindblom and Cohen (1980) call *ordinary knowledge*—including evaluative criteria and judgments about political feasibility. "Ordinary knowledge," according to Lindblom and Cohen

(1980, p. 12) is "knowledge that does not owe its origin, testing, degree of verification, truth status, or currency to distinctive [professional scientific inquiry] techniques but rather to common sense, causal empiricism, or thoughtful speculation and analysis." Lindblom and Cohen maintain that professional social scientists greatly overestimate the amount and distinctiveness of the information and analysis that they provide for social problem solving. Professional social scientists also greatly underestimate the society's use of existing and new "ordinary knowledge" from sources other than professional scientific inquiry.

Synthesizing Scientific and Ordinary Knowledge in Policy Analysis

The second study I worked on at OTA was a study of compensation for vaccine-related injuries. It illustrates how research brokering in the context of formative policy analysis can entail a synthesis of academic research findings and "ordinary knowledge" to reach policy conclusions. In the course of fulfilling a congressional committee request to offer options for the design of a vaccine injury compensation system, we made use of medical research literature on vaccine-related illnesses and side effects, an accounting firm's contract report to HEW on the frequency and range of medical costs associated with various types of serious vaccine injuries, the findings and recommendations of a British Royal Commission on a vaccine injury compensation system for the United Kingdom, statistics provided by the British government on outcomes of claims filed for vaccine-related injuries under the British system, published and unpublished papers by Center for Disease Control researchers on Japan's experience with mass influenza immunization and claims for compensation under Japan's vaccine injury compensation system, statistics from Center for Disease Control's (CDC) vaccine injury reporting system, a review of the legal literature on vaccine injury suits, and a National Science Foundation–sponsored study carried out by the Hastings Center on ethical issues in vaccine injury compensation—to name just a few of our sources.

Identifying Key Policy Questions. It is difficult to describe the methodology of focused synthesis in detail. It is difficult and it takes great skill to identify the appropriate policy-relevant questions (Patton, 1978). The importance of understanding how the problem is defined or perceived by various participants in the policy process—not only the policy makers, such as congressional committee members and staffs, but the various interest groups who will be affected by the policy—cannot be overestimated. "The definition and redefinition of a policy problem depend on the analyst's learning at the start the various definitions of the 'problem situation' that are held by significant participants. The analyst must learn to inquire directly and indirectly, to listen, and to read between the lines. He must judge what elements of a group's position are unalterable and which are possibly subject to bargaining or compromise. His choice is not only whether to work in a given problem area but how to reshape its definition in a way that is consistent with his capacities for analysis and with the expected response of the relevant actors to his proposals. The definition of the problem thus overlaps with the assessment of political feasibility" (McRae, 1980, p. 132).

The notion of including political feasibility in the definition of the problem could seem to compromise analytic objectivity. I am not suggesting that political considerations in the narrow partisan sense should be brought into the analysis. The broad issues of political feasibility that are of necessary and legitimate concern can best be discussed by example. When we were asked by a House committee to research the elements of a legislative proposal for a publicly funded vaccine injury compensation system, we realized early that one major concern of Congress was in keeping publicly funded vaccine injury compensation from setting a dangerous political precedent. Thus, a proposal for a publicly funded vaccine injury compensation system would not be politically feasible if the proposal made it difficult to justify refusing compensation to persons injured in the course of medical research or medical treatment or, indeed, by any product or service where injury was not the result of negligence or malicious intent. Clearly, the federal government could never afford to pay compensation to every American who suffered a no-fault injury not otherwise covered by insurance.

Rational Injury into Values. Accordingly, one essential requirement for the vaccine injury compensation system proposal seemed to be coherent philosophical principles for determining who would be compensated and why. More important, these philosophical principles had to be able to explain—persuasively—why government should assume responsibility of providing compensation for vaccine injuries but not for no-fault injuries in general.

For this reason, we developed a rationale for compensating vaccine injuries but not other types of no-fault injury. The rationale centered on the fact that government actively promotes, subsidizes, and, in such cases as compulsory vaccination prior to school entry, compels mass immunization. Moreover, mass immunization is promoted and subsidized by government, not only because it is good for the health of each individual, but also because it is in the public interest. As a result of herd immunity, a certain level of immunization in the community at large protects the unvaccinated, such as new-borns who are too young to receive the vaccine.

On these principles, not all vaccine injuries ought to be compensated. To warrant compensation, a vaccine injury must satisfy two criteria: It results from a vaccine actively promoted or mandated by government, and an element of public service as well as of private benefit is involved in taking the vaccine and thereby running the risk of vaccine-related injury. Accordingly, injuries resulting from rabies vaccine, which is administered after exposure to rabies, ought not to be compensated, because rabies vaccination in such cases is actually a medical treatment that only benefits the individual. Similarly, vaccines targeted at special populations, such as pneumoccocal vaccine, which is recommended only for the elderly and chronically ill, would seem to have a weaker claim for coverage, since they benefit only the individuals vaccinated, than DPT, polio, measles, mumps, and rubella vaccines, which provide the public benefit of herd immunity. Conversely, injuries from polio vaccine have perhaps the strongest claim to public compensation. That is, given the current high level of polio immunization in the population at large, the average American runs a greater risk of contracting polio as a result of the vaccine than of getting the disease naturally. Of course, if significant percentages of succeeding generations are not immunized, polio could again become epidemic. Thus, individuals who elect to run the risks of vaccine-related injury from polio immunization are primarily safeguarding the broad public interest of preventing future recurrence of epidemic polio.

We did not create this philosophical rationale for public compensation for vaccine injury out of whole cloth. Again, we acted as research brokers—interpreting the findings of academic study in a practical, policy-making context. Thus, in developing the principles, we drew heavily on a National Science Foundation–sponsored study by a philosopher at the Hastings Center (Gaskins, 1980) of the ethical issues raised by the swine flu affair.

Clearly, the development of a philosophical rationale for a publicly funded vaccine injury compensation system is not a scientific question. It is, however, an analytic task that can be addressed through rational inquiry, to which philosophers and ethicists might well be expected to contribute.

Although the term *evaluation* clearly derives from the root word *value,* rational inquiry into evaluative decisions in public policy is not typically considered to be part of the professional practice of evaluation research. For the research broker, who attempts to draw the policy-relevant meaning from social science research findings, however, evaluation—in the sense of awareness and weighing of alternative value positions—is an essential part of formative policy analysis.

Can Scientists Be Their Own Research Brokers?

In this chapter, I have used the example of two studies to describe the research brokering role that a congressional, scientific support agency like the Office of Technology Assessment can play in helping to bring scientific data and academic research findings into the policy-making process. I have discussed two tasks of the research broker in depth: critical evaluation of the claims to scientific authoritativeness of estimates, assertions, and data employed in policy debate, and focused synthesis of relevant research findings for purposes of formative policy analysis. One question remains to be answered. Can scientists act as their own research brokers, or does the role require a specialized organizational unit, such as the Office of Technology Assessment?

The literature on the use of evaluation research in policy making simply assumes that there is a direct relationship between the evaluation or policy researcher and the policy maker client. Thus, evaluation and other policy researchers are reminded that policy makers do not have time to read long reports, that they prefer one-page executive summaries of findings, and that they often prefer to be briefed orally rather than in writing.

In fact, there quite often is no direct relationship between researchers and policy maker clients. Studies nearly always have sponsors (that is, funding sources), but sponsors are not necessarily clients (that is, potential users of the research findings). Frequently, for example, policy-relevant research projects are sponsored by private foundations. Foundations may influence policy in some diffuse way, but they themselves are not policy makers. Similarly, many government agencies that fund research (for example, National Science Foundation, National Institute for Mental Health, National Center for Health Services Research) have few or no policy-making or operational responsibilities. My own research, which involved analysis of a sample of 300 research studies carried out by thirty different policy research institutes, suggests that academically based policy researchers are particularly likely to have structurally distant relationships with policy-making clients. This is partly because academic researchers prefer grants to contracts, partly because academic researchers are more likely than nonacademic research institutes or consulting firms to obtain funding from private foundations or government agencies that are primarily research-support rather than policy-making organizations, and partly because the thinking of academically based policy researchers is closer to basic research than the thinking nonacademic researchers (Doty and Marincek-Baer, in press).

The absence of a direct relationship between researchers and policy makers is even more striking with respect to Congress. With the notable exception of the National Academy of Sciences, Congress almost never commissions research directly from outside researchers. Instead, Congress requests a study by one of its support agencies or, more often, mandates the relevant executive-branch agency to carry out a study. In the latter case, agencies sometimes involve outside researchers in the study, but the researchers seldom if ever are given an opportunity to interact with congressional committees that are interested in the study. Rather, most of their interaction is with mid-level bureaucrats in the research component of the executive agency mandated to carry out the study. This means that it is structurally quite difficult for the academic researcher based outside Washington to broker research findings to policy makers. Most researchers lack a contact or entry point to the policy-making process. Clearly, most researchers do not want to wander the corridors of Washington trying to sell their research findings.

There are other barriers to scientists' acting as their own research brokers. First, few scientists are suited by training, custom, and perhaps temperament to the job. This has become especially obvious to me since I began to work as a policy analyst in a federal agency. In a typical two-hour briefing by evaluation researchers, they devote one hour and fifty minutes to explaining how the data were collected and analyzed and what techniques were employed to ensure validity and reliability. Findings and policy conclusions are not stated until the last ten minutes, when the researchers realize that they have almost run out of time. This suggests that it is the processes of research, not the findings, that impassion researchers. In particular evaluation researchers often seem most engaged by the technical challenges of making social research conform to the exacting standards of classical experimental design. Policymakers, in contrast, do not much care how findings were obtained so long as they can be trusted.

A second barrier to scientists' acting as their own research broker is the importance of timing in politics. It is vital to know how policy makers define the major issues at any given point in the policy process in order to know what types of knowledge can most usefully be brought to bear and in what form. This requires being on the spot or, at the very least, being on call to those who are in the political arena.

Although certain basic policy issues, such as cost, quality, and access to health care, tend to remain constant over long periods of time, how these issues are defined in the policy process changes greatly in just a few years or even just a few months. Yet, major evaluation research studies typically take several years to complete, and, in the meantime, politics may have caused the key policy questions to change. Five years ago, for example, passage of national health insurance seemed a definite possibility, and policy makers wanted to test some propositions germane to administering such a program. The results of these studies are just now becoming available. However, current interest centers on proposals promoting private market solutions and competition in health care financing. Thus, one key task of the policy analyst as research broker is to draw conclusions about current policy issues from studies that were designed to answer other questions. The changing definitions of policy problems and policy goals helps to explain why single studies rarely provide definitive answers to policy questions. Franklin Zweig (1979), a former staff member of the Senate Labor and Human Relations Committee, made this point very well: "Even when evaluators are careful to relate study objectives to policy issues (too infrequently the case according to many congressional staff), comparability among highly focused evaluation studies is so rare that congressional staff are faced with immense difficulties in relating studies at their margins. Until evaluations utilize policy analysis literature searches in designing evaluative research, this issue will not be remedied. Until the organizations funding, publishing, and disseminating evaluation reports aggregate studies by problem or policy issue and conduct secondary analyses linking studies within aggregated clusters, a foundation for creating comparability will not emerge. Until bureaucracies funding evaluative research require comparability with antecedent or concurrent studies in some form, the license to evaluate will not be channeled into a policy-functional literature" (Zweig, 1979, pp. 156–157). Yet, with the exception of a few evaluators who are pioneering meta-evaluations, most practicing scientists are interested in collecting and analyzing their own original data and reporting these results, not in doing interpretive syntheses.

For these and other reasons, my conclusion is that research brokering probably ought to be a separate specialty, not an activity performed by working scientists as an afterthought to their research. This is not to say that scientists should abandon the role entirely. Certainly, senior scientists often gravitate to the brokering role toward the end of their career. They bring prestige to the job and perform it exceptionally well. It should be clear, however, that research brokering is a time-consuming task. Perhaps the most compelling reason why research brokering should be a separate specialty is that the scientist who takes it seriously and gives it the time that it requires will have little time left for original research.

In my view, research brokering as a specialized function is only just emerging, and the social organization of this newly differentiated role is not yet clearly defined. The Office of Technology Assessment represents one organizational model but by no means the only one. Thus, I would like to leave the reader two questions to ponder: What organizational forms are most conducive to performance of the research brokering function, and what steps, if any, should evaluation researchers and other policy research-oriented scientists take to encourage further development of the brokering role?

References

Banta, D., and Behney, C. "Policy Formulation and Technology Assessment." *Milbank Memorial Fund Quarterly*, 1981, *59*, 445-479.

Coates, J. "Technology Assessment." In A. Teich (Ed.), *Technology and Man's Future*. New York: St. Martin's Press, 1977.

Coates, J. *Technology Assessment in Federal Agencies, 1971-1976*. Washington, D.C.: Program of Policy Studies in Science and Technology, George Washington University, 1979.

Doty, P., and Marincek-Baer, V. *Policy Research: An Empirical Test of a Conceptual Distinction*, in press.

Gaskins, R. "Equity in Compensation: The Case of Swine Flu." *Hastings Center Report, 10* (1), 1980.

Greenberg, W. (Ed.). *Competition in the Health Care Sector: Past, Present, and Future*. Washington, D.C.: Bureau of Economics, Federal Trade Commission, 1978.

Hadley, J., Holahan, J., and Scanlon, W. "Can Fee for Service Coexist with Demand Creation?" *Inquiry*, 1979, *16*, 247-258.

Hanft, R. S. "Use of Social Science Data for Policy Analysis and Policy Making." *Milbank Memorial Fund Quarterly*, 1981, *59*, 596-613.

Havelock, R. G. "Dissemination and Translation Roles." In T. L. Eidel and J. M. Kitchel (Eds.), *Knowledge Production and Utilization on Educational Administration*. Eugene: University of Oregon Press, 1968.

Lindblom, C., and Cohen, D. K. *Usable Knowledge*. New Haven, Conn.: Yale University Press, 1979.

MacRae, D. "Policy Analysis Methods and Governmental Functions." In S. Nagel (Ed.), *Improving Policy Analysis*. Beverly Hills, Calif.: Sage, 1980.

Meltzer, A. J. "Creating a Policy Analysis Profession." In S. Nagel (Ed.), *Improving Policy Analysis*. Beverly Hills, Calif.: Sage, 1980.

Merton, R. *Social Theory and Social Structure*. Glencoe, Ill.: Free Press, 1968.

Patton, M. Q. *Utilization-Focused Evaluation*. Beverly Hills, Calif.: Sage, 1978.

Reinhardt, U. *Physicians' Productivity and the Demand for Health Manpower: An Economic Analysis*. Cambridge, Mass.: Ballinger, 1975.

Rich, R. F. "Problem Solving and Evaluation Research." In R. F. Rich (Ed.), *Translating Evaluation into Policy*. Beverly Hills, Calif.: Sage, 1979.

Weiss, C. *Using Social Research in Public Policy Making*. Lexington, Mass.: Heath, 1977.

Welles, C. "Who Will Make Money in the '80s?" *Esquire*, 1980, *94*, 19-23.

Zweig, F. M. "The Evaluation World View of Congressional Staff." In F. Zweig (Ed.), *Evaluation in Legislation*. Beverly Hills, Calif.: Sage, 1977.

Pamela Doty was a 1979–1980 congressional fellow at OTA. Currently, she is a senior policy analyst in the Office of Legislation and Policy of the Health Care Financing Administration, the federal agency that administers Medicare and Medicaid. She is the author of Guided Change in the American Health System *(New York: Human Services Press, 1980).*

*The author reviews efforts of the 96th Congress to
use evaluation data in considering whether to
change policies about reimbursement for
psychotherapy services.*

Public Policy and Psychotherapy:
Can Evaluative Research
Play a Role?

Leonard Saxe

It is an understatement to note that the provision of psychotherapy
is a controversial issue (see, for example, the report of the President's
Commission on Mental Health, 1978). Although much of the recent
controversy has centered on public expenditures for psychotherapy,
the general nature and appropriateness of mental health treatments
has frequently been a volatile public policy concern.

Psychotherapy, along with other mental health treatments, is
practiced by professionals in medicine, psychology, and various social science and service disciplines. Perhaps psychotherapy incorpo-
rates the difficulties of each of the disciplines that train practitioners

This manuscript was completed during the author's appointment as a
Fulbright Lecturer in Psychology at the University of Haifa. Appreciation is expressed to the United States–Israel Binational Education Foundation and the
Department of Psychology at the University of Haifa for their support. The very
helpful comments of David Banta on an earlier draft of this manuscript are also
appreciated.

L. Saxe, D. Koretz (Eds.). *New Directions for Program Evaluation: Making Evaluation
Research Useful to Congress*, no. 14. San Francisco: Jossey-Bass, June 1982.

(Freud, 1937). During the last twenty to thirty years, both public and private mental health treatment systems have undergone dramatic changes. In part, these changes were the result of public policy decisions, although many resulted directly from research and practice innovations. This chapter reviews efforts in the 96th Congress to consider changing policies about reimbursement for psychotherapy services, based on evaluation data concerning the effects of psychotherapeutic treatment.

At the request of the Senate Labor and Human Resources Committee (Subcommittee on Health), the Office of Technology Assessment (OTA) prepared background paper entitled "The Efficacy and Cost-effectiveness of Psychotherapy" (Office of Technology Assessment, 1980b*) as part of a larger study of the cost-effectiveness of medical technology. The background paper was connected with the introduction of legislation designed to construct a reimbursement system based on efficacy and cost considerations. Traditionally, psychotherapy has received different treatment for reimbursement purposes than other health care interventions (DeLeon and VandenBos, 1980; McGuire, 1981). During the 96th Congress, pressures from professional groups and others to improve benefits for patients with mental disorders covered by Medicare or Medicaid (and, potentially, by a national health insurance program) led to reconsideration of this situation and to intense study of psychotherapy. The study was intended to address the conflict between those who believed that psychotherapy was necessary and humane and that it had positive economic benefits (for example, by reducing costs for general health care) and those who believed that psychotherapy was both inefficacious and potentially very costly.

The principal goal of this chapter is to assess congressional interest in and utilization of evaluative data. Thus, substantive issues about psychotherapy are reviewed only briefly. Much of the chapter is a case study, and as a result, the generalizability of this discussion to congressional use of evaluation is limited. First, the description of events is clearly selective, designed as it is to highlight certain hypotheses about how Congress operates and about how evaluative researchers can interact with the legislative system. Second, there are a number of idiosyncratic aspects to the situation, and the experience may not be generalizable to other congressional or policy-making situations. Thus, the implications of this analysis are probably more heuristic than concrete in their value for practicing evaluators.

*The OTA report is also referenced under the authors' names as: Saxe, L. (with B. Yates and F. Newman).

Genesis of the OTA Study

As described in the Editors' Notes, OTA's function as a congressional support agency is to assess the consequences of technological change and to consider the broad array of effects that can result from the application of scientific knowledge (Banta and Behney, 1981). Technology is broadly defined by the Congressional Board that oversees OTA, and many nonhardware technological applications are considered within the agency's purview. Almost from its inception in the early 1970s, OTA had on its staff a group of health experts who were concerned with assessing the effects of new and existing medical procedures or technologies. OTA's health group has studied and developed many reports both on general problems of medical technology (Office of Technology Assessment, 1976, 1978a) and on specific medical technologies (Office of Technology Assessment, 1977, 1978b).

In 1978, OTA began a major study of the cost-effectiveness of medical technology at the request of the Senate Human Resources Committee. The goal of the study was to examine the applicability of methods for assessing the cost-effectiveness and cost-benefit of medical technologies. The 1970s had witnessed rapid growth both in the number of new medical technologies and in the cost of health care. Congress was interested in determining the connection between these two events and in the use of methods, such as cost-effectiveness and cost-benefit analyses, to assess the increasingly large investments necessary to develop and employ sophisticated medical technology. In lay terms, there were two basic questions: Were the new investments in health technology providing acceptable payoffs, and were there more efficient ways of developing these technologies (OTA, 1980)?

While the study request came from the Senate Human Resources Committee, other committees were invited to cosponsor the project request. In this case, the Senate Finance Committee, then chaired by Senator Russell Long (its Health Subcommittee was chaired by Senator Herman Talmadge), sent a letter of support. In their letter, the committee and subcommittee chairs noted that several technologies were of particular importance to the Senate Finance Committee, and they requested that OTA prepare background papers on each of these technologies. One of the technologies was psychotherapy: The letter indicated that there were "over 130 psychotherapies" and that there was an urgent need to determine which of these were effective, which were ineffective, and which were reasonable, given their cost and particular outcomes.

This request was originated by the staff of the Senate Finance Committee, who felt that evaluations of the literature and testimony indicated that there were no controlled clinical studies of the efficacy, safety, and appropriateness of psychotherapy (Constantine, 1979; Marshall, 1980). The Senate Finance Committee was interested in developing legislation parallel to the Kefauver-Harris Act of 1962, which established procedures for evaluating drugs. Congress was under intense pressure to expand benefits for individuals with mental health problems. The Senate Finance Committee staff proposed to expand benefits only if expansion was warranted by evaluative data.

OTA was only one of a number of congressional groups and executive branch agencies (in particular, the Alcohol, Drug Abuse, and Mental Health Administration) that were asked to assess current knowledge about psychotherapy. These efforts were aimed both at helping the Senate Finance Committee to develop a legislative proposal and at assessing support in scientific and professional communities for specific legislative proposals affecting psychotherapy benefits. In part, OTA was asked to participate because the answers to congressional questions about psychotherapy could not be found directly in the extant literature, which appeared to provide inconsistent and contradictory assessments about the value of psychotherapy (Parloff, 1979). Scientists and professionals who testified before Senate and House committees were often harsh in their comments on proposals both for and against further public funding of psychotherapeutic treatments.

The request of the Senate Finance Committee for assessment of the available evaluation data on psychotherapy was not the result of ignorance. Although their definition of the problem was naive in some respects (as in the notion that there were "over 130 psychotherapies"), they had a very sophisticated view of the problems inherent in providing mental health services, and they were familiar with prominent aspects of the research literature (Eysenck, 1952; Smith and Glass, 1977). The committee held public hearings in 1978 on expansion of benefits for psychotherapy (DeLeon and VandenBos, 1980), at which a variety of witnesses—including researchers and clinicians from several of the psychotherapy disciplines—testified. The request for a systematic review of research evidence followed directly from questions about the appropriateness and effectiveness of psychotherapy raised at those hearings.

However, Senate Finance Committee members did not have a good understanding of the research process. They did not distinguish among basic research, applied research, evaluative data and program evaluation, nor did they have a good understanding of the implications of the use of various experimental and nonexperimental research designs. Whether evidence stems from basic or applied research may not make an important difference to congressional users, but knowledge of what types of questions can be answered by various forms of research is important. Based on their experience with other health care technologies, the committee was interested in applying "scientific criteria"—however that might be defined. It should also be noted that committee staff were frustrated by inconsistencies in previous testimony and skeptical that positive evidence for psychotherapy could be provided.

Study Design

In response to the Senate Finance Committee request, OTA was expected to produce a report, called a background paper because it was supposed to be ancillary to the main report, which assessed cost-effectiveness in medical technology. While the request implicitly required research, the intent was not for OTA to conduct original research. Instead, it was expected that OTA would synthesize available information and that this synthesis would reflect the best current judgments from scientists in fields relevant to psychopathology and its treatment. The term *study design* will be used to describe OTA's approach to the problem.

OTA's inhouse health staff was multidisciplinary, and several staff held multiple degrees (for instance, medicine-public health, medicine-law); however, none was an expert on mental health problems. The author, who was serving as a Congressional Fellow, came closest, as a social psychologist interested in the evaluation of social interventions. Although his interests were not directly in mental health, his methodological skills were germane. As is often the case in public policy settings, generic skills were seen as more important than content area expertise, and he was asked to develop the study with the backing of OTA's other health researchers.

It was clear that such issues as the intense interdisciplinary rivalry that existed among mental health professionals (particularly between medicine and psychology but also between these disciplines and social work and nursing) would have to be dealt with (Hogan, 1979). Not only were there intense debates about the appropriate role of particular professions, but theoretic and therapeutic approaches created major divisions within each professional group. To some extent, the mental health professions avoid conflict by having their own journals, their own professional meetings, and by engaging in private practice. Congressional debates, however, force various professional groups to deal with one another. As director of OTA's study, my advantage was that I was a researcher, not a clinician.

In developing the study design, we decided to have much of the basic data about the effectiveness of psychotherapy, particularly its cost-effectiveness, collected by independent contractors. OTA would organize the data-collection process and synthesize and evaluate the resulting data. The problem of selecting appropriate contractors was discussed with congressional staff (in the House and the Senate, the CBO, and the GAO), staff of several professional associations (including the American Psychological Association and the American Psychiatric Association), and the executive branch (National Institute of Mental Health). As a result of these discussions, a request for proposals (RFP) was developed. Because OTA, as a congressional agency, is not required to follow formal government rules about procurement, the RFP took the form of an outline of questions about psychotherapy. It was sent to approximately twenty groups of investigators (mostly interdisciplinary teams of psychologists and psychiatrists) for response. Six proposals were received. An ad hoc review committee composed of congressional staffers from OTA, relevant committees, and support agencies selected one.

The psychologists whose proposal was selected for funding (see Yates and Newman, 1980a, 1980b, for a full description of their work) were selected because they seemed best to understand the information needs of OTA and because of their particular expertise in cost-effectiveness assessment of psychotherapy. Cost-effectiveness and cost-benefit analyses of mental health treatments have been rare until recently, and few psychologists are steeped in economic theory well enough to deal with these issues. Yates and Newman were an exception in this regard.

A special advisory panel was established to review work on the project and to advise OTA on substantive issues of psychotherapy evaluation. The panel was meant to complement OTA's inhouse review and advisory process and to provide special expertise not available among members of a larger panel established to advise the general cost-effectiveness study. The special panel included seven members, all prominent contributors to the research literature and recent public policy debates about psychotherapy.*

In addition, observers from congressional committees and

---

*The members of the panel were Jerome D. Frank, Ph.D., M.D. (Johns Hopkins University), Donald Klein, M.D. (New York State Psychiatric Institute), Beverly Long (National Mental Health Association), Thomas McGuire, Ph.D. (Boston University), Morris Parloff, Ph.D. (National Institute of Mental Health), Hans Strupp, Ph.D. (Vanderbilt University), and Gary VandenBos, Ph.D. (American Psychological Association).

agencies were invited to each of the meetings and provided with draft documents. The advisory panel included two psychiatrists (one who also had a Ph.D. in psychology), two psychologists, an economist, and an officer of the National Mental Health Association (a citizen's group concerned with mental health services). The panel was balanced, not only by discipline but also (to the greatest extent possible) by research orientation.

The advisory panel met twice. In addition, its members were primary reviewers of preliminary drafts of the report. Much of the panel's advice served to point OTA to relevant sources. More importantly, panel members debated the strength of evidence about the effectiveness of psychotherapy and the acceptability of OTA's conclusions. The results of these discussions were not directly incorporated in the report, but they helped to shape its findings.

While the OTA report was being prepared, there was a great deal of related activity in Congress, especially among staff of the Senate Finance Committee. Legislation was drafted, and opinions were sought on an amendment to the Social Security Act modifying reimbursement policy for psychotherapy. At least in its early form, this amendment was modeled on legislation regulating drugs. The amendment proposed to establish a national commission to study psychotherapy over a three- to five-year period and make recommendations on reimbursement for psychotherapeutic treatments. The recommendations were on research evidence about the effectiveness of various treatments. Committee staff, of course, were not concerned with the theoretical nuances of evaluative research or cost-effectiveness and cost-benefit analyses. Their interest was in the bottom line—the degree to which psychotherapy yielded provable effects ("scientifically based," in their terms) at reasonable cost. Their decision needs were relatively clear-cut, and they were searching for a way to use evaluative data in the development of specific reimbursement policies.

One aspect of the legislative drafting work of the Senate Finance Committee staff was that they were primarily interested in efficacy questions, rather than cost-effectiveness. Partly as a result of their emphasis, the background paper (Office of Technology Assessment, 1980b) based on the contractors' report was larger than initially envisioned. While it focused principally on the conduct of effectiveness studies, it also considered the use of cost-effectiveness and cost-benefit analyses as a tool for aiding decisions about reimbursement policy for mental health services.*

---

*The report was reviewed and edited by OTA's in-house staff, as well as by panel members of the special advisory group and the advisory group and the advisory panel for the overall cost-effectiveness study.

Findings

A central tenet of those who developed the report (Office of Technology Assessment, 1980b) was that a balanced view of mental health treatments should be provided. No orientation was to be favored *a priori*, and the data were expected to guide the conclusions. It seemed inevitable that professionals, both researchers and practitioners, would disagree with at least some of the conclusions. Because OTA's stance as a nonpartisan agency, the report emphasized scientific criteria and did not make specific recommendations to Congress. Instead, the report described the problem and tried to summarize the available knowledge.

In its final form, the report discussed four issues related to assessment of psychotherapy: the definition and complexity of psychotherapy, the degree to which psychotherapy is amenable to scientific analysis, the evidence about the efficacy of psychotherapeutic treatments, and the appropriateness and results of cost-effectiveness and cost-benefit analysis of psychotherapy.

One principal difficulty in advising policy makers about psychotherapy is that it is not a simple treatment. Confusion about its effectiveness results, in part, from the different views of what comprises psychotherapy. A number of definitions of psychotherapy were summarized in the OTA report. Psychodynamic, behavioral, and so-called humanistic approaches were all considered and included as therapies, despite the important differences among them. One reason was that OTA staffers felt that the theoretical orientation of therapy was not its most important characteristic; there was substantial evidence that other factors affect outcomes in important ways. For example, therapist characteristics, patient characteristics, and aspects of the treatment setting can all affect therapeutic outcomes as much as theoretical orientation does.

In order to delineate the scientific basis of psychotherapy, the report described a series of methodological strategies underlying the design and analysis of psychotherapy outcome research. Because of the committee's interest in "scientific" analysis, one focus of the discussion was the conduct of true experiments (that is, randomized designs). The report discussed situations under which such experiments have been conducted and how they can be carried out to evaluate the effects of psychotherapy (Saxe and Fine, 1981). Use of quasi-experimental and nonexperimental procedures was also analyzed. Also considered was the ability of program evaluation to test the effects of particular combinations of psychotherapy variables. The use of systematic procedures, such as meta-analysis, for synthesizing the findings of multiple investigations was also reviewed (Wortman and Saxe, 1981).

For congressional users of the report, the most important section was probably the review of the literature on psychotherapy outcomes. Because of the size of the literature, the report focused on the most prominent reviews of the psychotherapy literature and on the commentary generated by these reviews. The central finding of the review was that, despite important differences in the criteria used in the literature for assessing psychotherapy outcomes, all reports seemed to provide some evidence of psychotherapy's effectiveness (Parloff, 1979; VandenBos and Pino, 1980). This finding is stronger when more recent literature is reviewed, and there is little evidence for the inefficacy of psychotherapeutic treatments. The report did not find other explanations, such as spontaneous remission and placebo effects, convincing. At the very least, the literature indicates that the promise of psychotherapy is still high and implies that a systematic research program linked to particular policy decisions is potentially useful.

The report found no fundamental problem in applying cost-benefit analysis to psychotherapy. Nevertheless, as with its application to other medical technologies, such analysis can yield misleading results (Office of Technology Assessment, 1980a). One problem posed by cost-benefit assessment of psychotherapy is that it is difficult to ensure that all the appropriate variables are being measured. Benefits are particularly difficult to measure comprehensively because of the difficult problem of translating psychological benefits, such as "happiness," into measurable terms. Also, there is relatively little good-quality empirical evidence about the cost-effectiveness or cost-benefit of psychotherapy, although such research is increasing. Before 1980, much of this research focused on low-cost interventions, where it is not necessary to measure benefits extensively in order to show positive effects for psychotherapy.

In sum, the report prepared by OTA (Office of Technology Assessment, 1980b) provided a moderately positive assessment both of the scientific basis for psychotherapy treatments and of the results of evaluative studies. Many congressional staffers working directly on this problem remained skeptical. However, the main message of the report—that the problem of psychotherapy is complex but that science does have methods to develop answers for such questions—was compatible with the world view held by many knowledgeable congressional staff people (Zweig, 1979).

Almost two years elapsed between the initial request to OTA and submission of the final document. Such a time span is not unusual for scholarly work or research. If anything, it is probably shorter than normal. In the context of congressional decision making, however, it is a long time, and it may only be luck that the report was available when debate took place.

Congressional Considerations

During the legislative session when the OTA reports were released, Senator Matsunaga, a member of the Senate Finance Committee, introduced legislation (S. 3029, 96th Congress) to amend the Social Security Act to form a national commission to assess the effectiveness of psychotherapy. The commission, to be funded with $20 million in Social Security funds, would have several years in which to make recommendations about the conditions under which psychotherapy treatments would be reimbursed for Medicare and Medicaid eligible patients. The commission was to be an interdisciplinary panel of physicians and behavioral scientists, divided between mental health practitioners and researchers. The panel would be charged with assessing current knowledge about the effects of particular treatment-patient interactions and, where data were unavailable, with funding new studies. The commission's findings were to be reflected in reimbursement policy at a later time.

Like most bills filed during a particular session of Congress, S. 3029 did not become law. Hearings were scheduled in September 1980, but they were cancelled when the chairman of the Health Subcommittee of the Senate Finance Committee was unable to attend because of a conflict with his re-election campaign schedule. Nevertheless, the bill was to have been considered on the Senate floor during the so-called lame duck session of Congress following the November 1980 elections. The House would then have been asked to concur, most likely during joint conference proceedings. Because of the election results, however, which passed control of the Senate from the Democrats to the Republicans, the interim session was devoted only to essential legislation, and S. 3029 was not considered.

Implications for the Use of Evaluative Data

Given that OTA's report did not result in the enactment of legislation, what can be said of congressional use of psychotherapy data? Two general observations are in order. First, the inaction had little to do with the substance of the psychotherapy problem. Although the bill would probably have been considered earlier had it not involved such a controversial issue and had mental health professionals been strong advocates, inaction resulted from the larger political context, not the legislation itself. In 1980, voters appeared to be reacting more to global economic problems than to expanding federal involvement in social programs.

Second, despite the lack of legislative action, there are a number of positive aspects of the situation for evaluators. It was clear from the beginning of OTA's involvement with the Senate Finance Committee that there was tremendous misinformation about psychotherapy. Unlike medical interventions, with which it is classified, psychotherapy has relatively subtle effects, and its failures are probably more obvious than its successes. With this in mind, and given the disagreements among professional groups about psychotherapy, it is perhaps not surprising that legislators view psychotherapy with skepticism. It leads them to interpret information about effects negatively (for example, to place more confidence in negative outcomes than in positive ones). What is significant is that data were requested at all and that Congress at least had available reviews of the scientific evaluation literature. That Congress had the ability to collect and synthesize such data should be welcome news to evaluators and other researchers who are concerned about whether policy makers pay attention to their work (Parloff, 1979).

The OTA experience also indicates that not only are evaluation data seen as useful, but they also can alter views of policy makers. The original drafts of S. 3029 were modeled on Federal Drug Administration legislation. Psychotherapies were classified (parallel to the system for drugs), and each treatment was to be scrutinized for evidence of clinical effects. One clear implication of the OTA report was that such an approach is inappropriate for psychotherapy. The report identified many other components of the therapeutic situation that affect treatment outcomes, and it implicitly clarified the problems raised by the view of psychotherapy as equivalent to a drug. OTA's input, not only the final report, but also memoranda and meetings, was only one of many channels through which those who drafted the legislation received information. The final form of the bill, however, included OTA's statement of the many variables that affect psychotherapeutic outcomes. In effect, the report changed how the question was framed.

This assessment of the role played by evaluation data may seem to contradict common wisdom about the use of evaluation by Congress (Cronbach and others, 1980). Commentators have tended to view evaluators as focused narrowly on a particular issue and as unwilling to take the broader concerns of Congress into consideration. In the present case, it is significant that the request for the study emanated directly from the interested congressional group and specifically focused on synthesizing available knowledge. In addition, the assessment was conducted not by an original researcher but by an analyst whose allegiance was to a congressional agency with the backing of a prestigious and independent panel. This combination of "ownership" of the study by the user with the presence of a research broker (see the chapter by Doty in this volume) was probably essential to the positive outcomes of this case study.

In addition to these two general observations, a number of lessons for evaluators can be drawn from this case study.

Implicit Use of Evaluation. Although evaluation research as most social scientists define it is not widely employed by Congress, its use seems implicit in the process of congressional decision making. Evaluative data can be called for informally, as when a request is made for information (for example, to the Congressional Reference Service) about the facts of a problem, or the request can be made formally, as when the General Accounting Office is asked to perform an evaluation (Chelimsky, 1981). Formal evaluation, however, goes by many names on Capitol Hill, including *technology assessment, social experimentation,* and *program evaluation.* It is important to recognize how evaluation appears to legislators and the special needs of the congressional audience—particularly its need for syntheses, rather than individual studies. Probably the key to effective use of formal evaluation is knowledgeable staff, who can both request and interpret the vast array of information typically available.

Methodological Rigor. Members of Congress and by extension their staff cannot be expected to be knowledgeable about the intricacies of evaluation and research design. This does not mean, however, that evaluations must be simple or that they do not need to be methodologically sound. In the case described here, availability of rigorous, controlled research on the effects of psychotherapy was essential. Such data both blunted ad hominem arguments that impugned the scientific respectability of psychotherapy research and contributed substantially to the rejection of alternative explanations. Legislative reviewers seem to need reassurance from authoritative sources that data are reliable. Methodological rigor is reassuring.

Patterns of Data. Perhaps the most important feature of the OTA report was that it summarized extant reviews of the evaluation literature on psychotherapy. Because psychotherapy has been a controversial policy area, and because it has generated a prodigious research literature, policy makers needed assistance in interpreting competing claims. This is why syntheses of the literature, such as Smith, Glass, and Miller's (1980) meta-analytic assessment, received prominent attention. Such meta-analyses allow trends to be seen and the biases and selective problem focus of individual evaluators to be dealt with. While it is possible that meta-analytic methods only compound errors built into individual studies and reviews, meta-analyses seem a much more acceptable risk than review of selected individual studies.

Final Comments

One finding of the OTA report was that the effectiveness of therapy may be related to "nonspecific" factors. These factors refer to the way in which the therapist interacts with the patient (for example, with understanding and respect). Perhaps this explanation of psychotherapeutic effectiveness can provide a metaphor for congressional use of evaluation. Evaluation cannot play an effective role in the congressional process unless evaluators establish a significant relationship with the shapers of legislation. The specifics of the legislative problem and the evaluation solution may be less important than the process by which evaluation is presented to Congress.

While it is unrealistic for most evaluators personally to develop a significant relationship with legislative decision makers, this should not diminish the importance of considering the congressional audience. Congress needs evaluative data. It will use whatever it has at hand. To the extent that evaluators continue to conduct research on problems that are important to society and to the extent that they are honest both about the conclusions and the implications, evaluation research is potentially very valuable. With the help of knowledgeable congressional staff, such work can help to improve both the level of discourse about national policy and the policies themselves.

References

Banta, H. D., and Behney, C. J. "Policy Formulation and Technology Assessment." *Milbank Memorial Fund Quarterly,* 1981, *51,* 445-479.

Chelimsky, E. "Designing Backward from the End-Use." Presidential address to the Evaluation Research Society, October 1981.

Constantine, J. Letter to Dr. Gerald L. Klerman, administrator, Alcohol, Drug Abuse, and Mental Health Administration, November 15, 1979.

Cronbach, L. J., Ambron, S. R., Dornbush, S. M., Hess, R. D., Hornik, R. C., Phillips, D. C., Walker, D. F., and Weiner, S. S. *Toward Reform of Program Evaluation: Aims, Methods, and Institutional Arrangements.* San Francisco: Jossey-Bass, 1980.

DeLeon, P. H., and VandenBos, G. R. "Psychotherapy Reimbursement in Federal Programs: Political Factors." In G. R. VandenBos (Ed.), *Psychotherapy: Practice, Research, Policy.* Beverly Hills, Calif.: Sage, 1980.

Eysenck, H. "The Effects of Psychotherapy: An Evaluation." *Journal of Consulting Psychology,* 1952, *16,* 319-324.

Freud, S. "Analysis, Terminable and Interminable." *International Journal of Psychoanalysis,* 1937, *18,* 373-405.

Garfield, S. L. "Psychotherapy: A Forty-year Appraisal." *American Psychologist,* 1981, *36,* 174-183.

Hogan, D. B. *The Regulation of Psychotherapists: A Study in the Philosophy and Practice of Professional Regulations.* Cambridge, Mass.: Ballinger, 1979.

Marshall, E. "Psychotherapy Faces Test of Worth." *Science*, 1980, *207*, 35–36.

McGuire, T. *Psychotherapy and National Health Insurance: Issues and Evidence.* Cambridge, Mass.: Ballinger, 1981.

Office of Technology Assessment. *Development of Medical Technology: Opportunities for Assessment.* Washington, D.C.: U.S. Government Printing Office, 1976.

Office of Technology Assessment. *Development of Medical Technology: Opportunities for Assessment.* Washington, D.C.: Government Printing Office, 1976.

Office of Technology Assessment. *Cancer Testing Technology and Saccharin.* Washington, D.C.: U.S. Government Printing Office, 1977.

Office of Technology Assessment. *Assessing the Efficacy and Safety of Medical Technologies.* Washington, D.C.: U.S. Government Printing Office, 1978a.

Office of Technology Assessment. *Policy Implications of the Computed Tomography (CT) Scanner.* Washington, D.C.: U.S. Government Printing Office, 1978b.

Office of Technology Assessment. *The Implications of Cost Effectiveness Analysis of Medical Technology.* Washington, D.C.: U.S. Government Printing Office, 1980a.

Office of Technology Assessment. *The Efficacy and Cost-Effectiveness of Psychotherapy. Background Paper #3, Cost-Effectiveness of Medical Technology.* Washington, D.C.: U.S. Government Printing Office, 1980b.

Parloff, M. B. "Can Psychotherapy Research Guide the Policymaker? A Little Knowledge May Be a Dangerous Thing." *American Psychologist*, 1979, *34*, 296.

Patton, M. Q. *Utilization-Focused Evaluation.* Beverly Hills, Calif.: Sage, 1978.

President's Commission on Mental Health. *Report to the President.* Vol. 1. Washington, D.C.: U.S. Government Printing Office, 1978.

Saxe, L., and Fine, M. *Social Experiments: Methods for Design and Evaluation.* Beverly Hills, Calif.: Sage, 1981.

Smith, M. L., and Glass, G. V. "Meta-Analysis of Psychotherapy Outcome Studies." *American Psychologist*, 1977, *32*, 752.

Smith, M. L., Glass, G. V., and Miller, T. I. *The Benefits of Psychotherapy.* Baltimore, Md.: Johns Hopkins University Press, 1981.

VandenBos, G. R., and Pino, C. D. "Research on the Outcome of Psychotherapy." In G. R. VandenBos (Ed.), *Psychotherapy: Practice, Research, Policy.* Beverly Hills, Calif.: Sage, 1980.

Wortman, P. M., and Saxe, L. "The Assessment of Medical Technology: Methodological Considerations." Monograph prepared for the Office of Technology Assessment, 1981.

Yates, B. T., and Newman, F. L. "Approaches to Cost-Effectiveness Analysis and Cost-Benefit Analysis of Psychotherapy." In G. R. VandenBos (Ed.), *Psychotherapy: Practice, Research, Policy.* Beverly Hills, Calif.: Sage, 1980a.

Yates, B. T., and Newman, F. L. "Findings of Cost-Effectiveness and Cost-Benefit Analysis of Psychotherapy." In G. R. VandenBos (Ed.), *Psychotherapy: Practice, Research, Policy.* Beverly Hills, Calif.: Sage, 1980b.

Zweig, F. M. "The Evaluation World View of Congressional Staff." In F. M. Zweig (Ed.), *Evaluation in Legislation.* Beverly Hills, Calif.: Sage, 1979.

Leonard Saxe is assistant professor of psychology at Boston University.

Index

A

Academic researchers, and policy process, 62–63, 67–68
Access to evaluation research by Congress, 27
Advisory panels, 62–63, 78–79
Aherback, J. D., 8
Aid to Families with Dependent Children (AFDC), 34
Alcohol, Drug Abuse, and Mental Health Administration (ADAM-HA), 76
Ambron, S. R., 85
American Association for the Advancement of Science (AAAS), 1, 7
American Coalition of Citizens with Disabilities (ACCD): evaluation report on accessibility regulations, 12, 14–15, 18, 20, 22–23; rebuttal to Congressional Budget Office cost analysis, 17, 18, 23
American Council of the Blind, 15
American Medical Association (AMA), 56
American Psychiatric Association, 78
American Psychological Association, 78
American Public Transit Association v. *Lewis*, 15, 16, 21, 23
Armstrong, W., 17
Assumptions in forecasting, 61–62

B

Banta, D., 53, 70, 73*n*, 85
Behney, C. J., 53, 70, 85
Bi-State Development Corporation, 12
Bronfenbrenner, U., 43, 49
Brown, S., 5, 9–24, 10, 23, 27, 29
Bureau of Health Manpower estimates of physician supply and requirements, 55, 56–58

C

Capitation grants, 53–55
Carter administration, 11, 15, 35
Center for Disease Control (CDC), 64
Chelimsky, E., 84, 85
Cleveland, J., 16, 17, 18, 19
Coates, J., 53, 70
Cohen, D. K., 63, 70
Committees. *See* Congressional committees
Common sense, 63
Comptroller General, 4
Congress, U.S.: access to evaluation, 27; communicating study results to, 22, 26, 33–34, 39, 45–48, 53–54, 62; concern with setting precedents, 65; control of funding of evaluation research, 28–29; key themes of, 22–23; *97th*, 32, 36–41, 43, 45, 54, 56, 82; *96th*, 1–5, 11, 15–19, 44, 54, 73–85; and outside researchers, 68; reliance on Congressional Budget Office cost analyses, 20, 21; structure of, 2; use of evaluation research by, 25, 26, 74, 82–85
Congressional Budget and Impoundment Control Act of 1974, 4
Congressional Budget Office (CBO), 6, 12, 23, 29, 78; analyses of Professional Standards Review Organization program by, 35, 38–41, 43, 44; cost analysis of implementing Department of Transportation accessibility regulations, 11–15, 16–17, 18, 20, 22; evaluation reports, acceptance by Congress, 20, 21; functions of, 3, 4–5; publicizing findings of, 21–22
Congressional committees: appropriations, 35, 36; formal hearings of, 27–28; functions of, 2; oversight, 35, 36; pace of work of, 31; re-

87

Williams, H., 18
Wortman, P. M., 80, 86

Y

Yates, B., 74*n*, 78, 86

Z

Zigler, E. F., 42, 50
Zorinsky, E., 18
Zweig, F., 27, 47, 50, 69, 70, 81, 86